Quarterl

"When I read the book *Quarterlife Crisis,* I wept. . . . They pinned the tale on the donkey. Even those who don't recognize the term relate to it." —*The Toronto Star*

"In *Quarterlife Crisis,* Ms. Robbins, 25, outlined the distinction between her generation's crisis points and those of her parents' generation." —*New York Times*

"*Quarterlife Crisis* is a good place for recent graduates to turn for inspiration and reassurance." —*Columbus Dispatch*

"*Quarterlife Crisis* . . . caused a global sensation."
—*Straits Times*

"The catch phrase du jour and the title of the latest generational treatise—'Quarterlife Crisis'—has spawned a national dialogue." —*Los Angeles Times*

Conquering Your
Quarterlife
Crisis

Advice from
Twentysomethings
Who Have Been There
*and **Survived***

Alexandra Robbins

A PERIGEE BOOK

A Perigee Book
Published by The Berkley Publishing Group
A division of Penguin Group (USA) Inc.
375 Hudson Street
New York, New York 10014

Copyright © 2004 by Alexandra Robbins
Cover design by Ben Gibson
Text design by Julie Rogers

First Perigee paperback edition: October 2004

ISBN 0-399-53038X

Visit our website at
www.penguin.com

Library of Congress Cataloging-in-Publication Data

Robbins, Alexandra, 1976-
    Conquering your quarterlife crisis: advice from twentysomethings who have been there and survived / Alexandra Robbins.—1st Perigee pbk. ed.
        p. cm.
    "A Perigee book."
    ISBN 0-399-53038-X
    1. Young adults—Life skills guides. 2. Young adults—Attitudes. 3. Young adults—Conduct of life. I. Title

HQ799.5.R63 2004
305.235—dc22   2004044572

PRINTED IN THE UNITED STATES OF AMERICA

10   9   8   7   6   5   4   3   2   1

Dedicated with love to
Missy, Andrew, Jo, Ira, Dave, Irving, Rachel, Marty, and Seena

Contents

For additional advice, many more stories and suggestions, information for Quarterlife Crisis support groups and mentor programs, or to schedule a lecture or appearance by Alexandra Robbins, please visit *www.alexandrarobbins.com.*

Introduction

The answers

Three years ago, a little book called *Quarterlife Crisis* unexpectedly hit a big nerve. The book described the feelings of apprehension and indecision that walloped twentysomethings during the transition between young adulthood and adulthood. It discussed how twentysomethings were lost and confused, largely because there was no road map to these years, no manual providing answers. It lamented the absence of a guide—a book with solutions for how to emerge successfully and happily from the struggles of this age.

Conquering Your Quarterlife Crisis is that guide.

This new book is written for all twenty- and thirtysomethings, regardless of gender, finances, race, status, and geographic location. It is for, and includes advice from, those who went to college, as well as those who did not; those who work blue-collar jobs, white-collar jobs, or no job at all; those with money and those carrying six-figure debt loads; those with relatively few obligations and those who are single parents with tremendous responsibilities; and those who are close to depression and those who feel like they almost have it together. *Conquering Your Quarterlife Crisis* addresses our age group's common bond: the deep, soul-searching questions that keep us awake at night; the tough, hard-hitting questions that we're sometimes too afraid to ask even ourselves.

Many of us in our twenties and thirties go through a period that leaves us feeling panicked or directionless. For some of us, the challenges of this time become so overwhelming that we may seriously second-guess our abilities, intensely question our lives, or crush our own self-esteem with our doubts. That's what happened to me. I wrote the first *Quarterlife Crisis* essentially to figure out what was so wrong with me that during what I thought were supposed to be the most carefree, freewheeling years of my life, I felt useless, sad, and ill equipped for life after school.

But something happened during the process of writing that first book that changed my life. As I interviewed twentysomething after twentysomething, in the course of compiling other people's stories, my own story changed. After months of regularly beating myself to a mental pulp because I wasn't living up to my own standards, it was the simplest of facts that jolted me out of my funk: I was normal. When the twentysomething sources unloaded on me their fears, doubts, and uncertainties, I realized that my insecurities were common—and that I therefore wasn't a freak after all. That was all I needed to know.

I have heard from hundreds of readers who only needed to know the same thing. But countless more twentysomethings wrote to tell me that simply knowing their problems were normal didn't solve them. Over the past three years, scores of readers have pointed out that there was something missing from the book *Quarterlife Crisis,* an egregious omission that left them still searching, still questioning, still brokenhearted by the gap between the person they are and the person they want to be.

The book was missing the answers.

When I started writing that first book, I was 23 and in the midst of my own Quarterlife Crisis. I thought it would be presumptuous to offer my peers suggestions for how to fix their lives when I was so frustrated with my own. Other than sharing sources' stories with readers to let them know they weren't alone, I had no idea how else I could help them. But that was then.

I'm still not foolish enough to presume I have all the answers now. But thousands of other twentysomethings do, and I've spent the past few years grilling them for these solutions. That's what this book is for. While the point of the first book was to introduce the problems of the Quarterlife Crisis, the aim of *Conquering Your Quarterlife Crisis* is to solve them.

You don't need to have read that first book to get the most out of this one. The new premise of *Conquering Your Quarterlife Crisis* is that one of the major reasons our generation feels clueless and torn is that we don't have any mentors. Throughout our years in school, we had specific people to turn to for help and guidance: teachers, advisers, counselors, coaches, and parents. But once we graduate and grapple with real-world issues, we don't have someone readily available to tell us, "I've been there. Here's how I got through it." And because of the ever-widening generation gap, our parents' experiences in many areas aren't necessarily relevant anymore.

Take the workplace. Several decades ago, for example, a young graduate might have expected to choose a company and remain there for much of his or her life, gaining guidance and insights under the tutelage of older employees. Now, however, many workers view twentysomethings as threats to their jobs; instead of mentoring young hires, they often clash with or ignore them. This sense of competition has left our craving for guidance, at the workplace and in other areas of life, unfulfilled.

One of my aims with this book is to get the concept of mentorship back into society. Imagine if we each had people whom we could contact for advice whenever we had questions about work, love, dreams, home, social life, or identity issues—people who had wrestled with the same matters during similar times and conquered them. Imagine if we each had go-to guys who would talk us through hard times or, when we needed it, would give us a figurative kick in the pants. Imagine having your own personal Oprah. Your own personal Vince Lombardi.

The structure of this book mirrors that premise by providing those missing mentors, at least temporarily. After thousands of interviews, I've pinpointed some of the most widespread quarterlife dilemmas and paired twentysomethings in the midst of them with people in our generation who have dealt with those same situations successfully. For every twentysomething with a problem, I have twenty- or thirtysomethings with answers. I thought it was important that the voices of wisdom in this book come not from professional experts but from people who navigated these issues sometime over the past ten years. In fact, along with many new voices of experience, some of the original *Quarterlife Crisis* twentysomethings are back—older, wiser, healthier, and ready to serve as mentors. These mentors share the problems they faced, the suggestions they learned, and the advice they wish they had known. *Conquering Your Quarterlife Crisis* is the chance for our generation to get advice from people who have been there and done that.

It's probably too idealistic to hope that this book sparks the beginnings of a societal movement toward mentorship. It might be too cheesy to explicitly call for that. (Our generation isn't the "let's all hold hands and sing" type, anyway.) But how many times do we have to hear that we're an aloof generation before we do something about it? There are many reasons that we are an age group on disconnect, as Oprah rightly assessed in her show on the "Turbulent Twenties." But part of the responsibility to remedy that is on us. If we want to show older groups that we *do* care, that we *want* to lead a useful, helpful existence, perhaps it's time that we as a generation begin to combat that image.

It wouldn't hurt to start by reaching out to ask for help. Although in this book I use only fellow twenty- and thirtysomethings as mentors, in life there is nothing to lose by developing mentor relationships at any age. One might ask what older mentors would get out of this relationship beyond a sense of volunteerism and companionship. Actually, "reverse mentorship" is an idea that hasn't received much attention beyond a focus on technology training. Reverse mentors, usually twentysomethings, provide older individuals with insight into current popular culture and social trends, technological expertise, and generational thinking. Reverse mentorship programs have already caught on at some companies, including General Electric, Proctor & Gamble, and Best Buy. Just as mentorship plays a crucial role in this book, so, too, should it become an integral part of our lives. If we can return the workplace and social environment to one of mentorship—or fuel a new trend toward reciprocal relationships of mutual mentorship—we may collectively be able to conquer the Quarterlife Crisis once and for all.

To further bridge the generation gap, it helps to try to understand it. We live in completely different times than even our parents' generation. Our lifestyle, for example, is much more fast paced. Because the Internet Age affected our formative years, we have witnessed a hurtling pace of technological advance that has put a greater emphasis on quickness and convenience in our lives. From cell phones to instant messaging, microwaves to palm pilots, MP3s to DVDs, we have become not only accustomed to but even societally influenced to crave instant gratification. So perhaps it's not so surprising that when we consider our possible paths in life, we become anxious if we can't figure out ways to find and follow them quickly.

We also seem to be a much more introspective generation than older groups, if only because we are one of the first generations to have the luxury to do so. When older generations reached their 20s, they graduated from school, quickly looked for a life partner (if they hadn't found one already), and immediately leapt into a career to support the family they anticipated having soon. The 20s were not a time of trial and error, as they are for us. They were a time to grow up fast.

Many older people haven't realized that the twenties aren't what they used to be. For us, the twenties have become more of a transition period than an endgame. The average age of marriage has shifted from 21 for women and 23 for men in 1970 to 25 for women and 27 for men. The average number of jobs a person has in his or her 20s has jumped to 8.6 between the ages of 18 and 32, according to the U.S. Bureau of Labor Statistics. The phrase "30 is the new 20" has caught on.

While critics point to these figures as evidence of our generation's immaturity, I think they indicate something far more hopeful. Because we're not thrust into full-fledged adulthood immediately following adolescence, we are lucky enough to have the time and leisure to grapple with identity issues at a much earlier age than did members of the generations before us. This doesn't doom us to a lifetime of crises complaints, as critics have snarled. Rather, we are resolving in our twenties the issues that our parents didn't have time to wrestle with until middle age. This could mean that by the time our generation reaches middle age, because we will already have confronted our demons, we could escape the midlife crisis altogether. And by then, the notion that twentysomethings confront a tough phenomenon called the Quarterlife Crisis will hopefully be so widely accepted that little books introducing the concept will be beside the point.

Quarterlife Crisis FAQ

Whether this is the first you've heard of the Quarterlife Crisis or you'd simply like a refresher, here's all you need to know:

Q: *What is the Quarterlife Crisis?*

A: Like the midlife crisis, the Quarterlife Crisis is a response to reaching a turning point in life—in this case, the transition between young adulthood and adulthood. The overwhelming identity issues of this age can cause a variety of reactions, ranging from intense self-doubt that can spiral into something as serious as a clinical depression to something as subtle as looking at your life as an alleged adult and having a nagging feeling of "Is this all there is?"

These feelings can start as early as late adolescence, when you're nearing the end of your school years and preparing for the "real world," whether you're in high school or college. An upcoming graduation often triggers this kind of panic about your future; it's a natural fear of the impending culture shock. After we leave the school environment, suddenly there's no road map anymore. There are no promises that we can get from point A to point B, no matter how hard we work.

For other people, the Quarterlife Crisis hits in the mid-20s, when you feel that your life so far as a supposed adult isn't bringing you the satisfaction and inner peace you had expected. And for still others, the Quarterlife Crisis hits in the late twenties or early thirties, at around the time society somehow seems to expect us to have our lives all figured out.

Q: *What are some signs of the Quarterlife Crisis?*

A: Twentysomethings and thirtysomethings individually experience the Quarterlife Crisis in so many ways that it would be impossible to list them all here. Nonetheless, here are six relatively common signs:

1. **You don't know what you want.** One major cause of anxiety is that twentysomethings are afraid that we're not going to find the passion in life that inspires us, whether it's a job, a hobby, or a person. You worry that not only are you not going to be able to figure out how to get what you want, but also that you might not discover what it is you really want in the first place.

2. **Your 20s aren't what you expected.** We expect that our college and postcollege years will be the most carefree, responsibility-free time of our independent adult lives. But then when you are sitting alone at home, thinking that everyone else your age has it together while you're missing your friends from school, wondering how to find a date, and realizing you have no idea what

you want to do with your life, you feel like your uncertainties and doubts mean that there's something wrong with you.

3. You have a fear of failure. Another sign of a Quarterlife Crisis is a fear of failure—that if you fail at one thing, you'll fail at another, and your self-esteem will plummet.

4. You can't let go of childhood. You feel stuck in a limbo somewhere between young adulthood and adulthood, and you don't know how or when to let go of your childhood, or if you even want to.

5. You waffle over decisions. You're afraid that the choices you make now will put you on a path that will affect the rest of your life, and that if you make a mistake now, you won't be able to repair it later.

6. You constantly compare. You compare yourself to your peers and feel like you come up short. It's like attending a high school reunion, year after year after year. You're constantly measuring yourself, whether it's against your friends or against the standards you set up for yourself, however unreasonable they may be.

Q: *How is it different from a midlife crisis?*

A: The Quarterlife Crisis and the midlife crisis are both responses to reaching an age-related transition period. But while the resulting distress and confusion might be similar, the causes of these crises are opposite. At middle age a guy might feel his life is stagnant, with too much predictability, stability, and certainty. At 25, however, a common feeling is that there's too much *un*predictability, *in*stability, and *un*certainty.

I call it the Quarterlife Crisis simply because I think this phenomenon should be as widely acknowledged and accepted as the midlife crisis. The midlife crisis is a popularly accepted phenomenon that has spawned scores of resources to help middle-aged people transition and cope. I believe that people who experience the Quarterlife Crisis deserve just as many resources and reassurance that what they are going through is normal and fixable.

Q: *What if people say we're whining?*

A: It tends to be the people in the throes of a midlife crisis who are most vocally skeptical of the Quarterlife Crisis. These are the people who say things like, "You're young, you're educated, you have your whole life in front of you. What do *you* have to complain about?" When older people dismiss the idea of a Quarterlife Crisis as the undeserved complaints of a coddled postadolescent, they only exacerbate the problem. Depression and anxiety disorders are serious. When people our age are told that we can't be depressed because there's nothing seriously wrong in our lives, we are even more likely to think there's something wrong with us for feeling this way.

Part 1

Hopes and Dreams

These issues cut to the core of who we are and who we want to be. That's why most Quarterlife Crises begin with questions like, What if I don't know what I want? How do I find my passion? When do I let go of my dream? and How do I start over again?

The way you respond to your hopes and dreams now—whether you doggedly stifle them or relentlessly chase them, whether you meld into your life or pursue them with blinders blocking out everything else—can set a precedent for how you do so throughout your adulthood. Notice that I didn't say the way you *fulfill* your hopes and dreams. In your 20s, it's the process of reacting to them, rather than the success in pursuing them, that counts.

I chose to begin with this section on hopes and dreams because the mentors' suggestions are so insightful and the advice so varied, precise, and wise, that it would be difficult for you to read through it without discovering something—some nugget, idea, or truth—that will help you to make your life better. Perhaps you might find that one of the exercises, some of which could lead to overnight solutions, ignites the spark that tells you which direction to take. Or maybe one of the mentors' stories will inspire you to stop shuffling with hesitation and finally make the move that will change your life.

Chapter 1

What if I don't know what I want?

After graduating in 2001 with a liberal arts degree and no idea what to do with her life, Angelina Douglas* accepted a job as a dog walker. "Dog walking is very conducive to conversation with strangers, and I ended up talking with lots of random people whom I otherwise would not have met. Within the first three minutes of any discussion, I'd be justifying myself to these strangers, squeezing into the conversation that I had just graduated from college, and that this was just a temporary job, not a career. 'Post-college-life-experience.' 'Time to reflect.' 'Just 'til I figure out what I really want to do,' I told them. I liked dog walking itself, but I hated the way I felt when I was asked, 'So, what do you do?'" Angelina says. "When May came around and it had been a year after graduation, I still had no idea what to do with my life, but I could no longer say, 'I just graduated in May.' I felt tremendous pressure to do something real, something with my degree, something where I wasn't allowed to wear just shorts and a sports bra and throw tennis balls in the park, something that wouldn't give me a tan. So I quit dog walking and spent the

*Some names have been changed.

next year sampling 'grown-up jobs' that weren't taking me anywhere."

When she reached her two-year graduation anniversary, Angelina "finally gave in" and decided to get her master's degree in education. "It seemed like the only option. Although animals are my passion, there aren't real animal careers out there besides veterinary medicine, and that's just too overwhelming to even consider. I have very mixed feelings about being in grad school for education. I know it's not what I really want to do, but I don't know what it is that I really want to do. I'm tired of wandering aimlessly, wasting my life, so I guess I'd rather take a direction, any direction, even the wrong direction—at least I know where I'm going. I guess I'm not as free spirited as I once was, or as I'd like to think I was. I know I'm settling, and it pisses me off because I only have one life, and I should use it doing something that's more fulfilling for me. I use plenty of methods to try to manipulate my mind and rationalize all this. I tell myself that maybe when I begin teaching, I'll discover that I actually love it and take advantage of all the creative possibilities it offers me. Sometimes I remind myself that most people hate their job, and it's being happily in love that matters most, which I am, and never thought I would be. But sometimes I catch myself having retirement fantasies—going to every single major league ballpark, moving to New Zealand, owning a parrot and a monkey and an iguana—and that scares me, that I have to look forward to the final part of my life to do that."

Andro Hsu, a 27-year-old Californian, says he has been struggling with the question, What if I don't know what I want? for the majority of his life. "I've never really had a clear ambition for a career or my future self-image. Mostly it's been because of the paralysis of indecision. I feel I've had, if anything, too many choices in life, too much potential, and too little focus. As you go through that cynical phase all too common to twentysomethings, you get really good at coming up with reasons not to do things. Reasons why certain careers are 'selling out,' or ignoble, or don't offer enough freedom. The pain comes when you think you don't like what you're currently doing because your potential could be better realized by changing what you're doing, but then you've come up with all these reasons not to change what you're doing," Andro says. "I know it seems odd to be saying this when I'm in a six-year doctoral program, but I've arrived where I am mostly through surfing the waves of circumstance, making choices based on what seems logical, not out of any passionate desire. My original intent (which itself was derived out of parental pressure) was to go to medical school, but I got rejected by thirty of them. Since I had a biology degree, I thought it would be easiest to work for a biotech company. I don't know why it never occurred to me to try something new, like teaching or the Peace Corps. When I got completely fed up with the work I did and the company I worked for, I thought grad school would be appropriate because I already had a background in biology and biotechnology. Again, the deferred choice."

Take Risks

MENTOR: Gwen Snyder
AGE: 32

I WISH I'D KNOWN AT 22 THAT "you should take risks but make them well defined, to decrease the likelihood of hardships that would discourage you from future risks."

When Gwen Snyder graduated from Hope College, she didn't know what she wanted to do. Her only lead was that in the poor job market at the time, she realized that in whatever career she would eventually choose, she would be more marketable if she spoke a foreign language fluently.

Three weeks after graduation, Gwen moved alone to Santiago to do research for a professor from college. When Gwen completed the research, she decided to stay longer. Over the next year and a half, she worked as an English teacher and business consultant and befriended a Chilean woman who took her under her wing. By the time Gwen left Chile, she was fluent in Spanish, could cook

Chilean, had learned to salsa, and knew exactly what she wanted to do with her life: to work to improve Latin American policy and economics. "The experience put Latin America in my blood," Gwen says. "After returning to the States, I was an assistant trade advisor on the State of Ohio International Trade Division's Latin America desk. That experience qualified me to apply for a multi-country Fulbright Scholarship in Argentina and Brazil researching international trade. That led to a master's degree from Johns Hopkins in Latin American economics. All of this stemmed from the risk I took in moving alone to Chile when I was 22."

Gwen's advice to twentysomethings who don't know what they want is to take risks. Immediately. "A group of 80-year-olds was asked, 'Looking back on your life, what would you do differently?' Their number one answer was, 'I would take more risks,'" Gwen says. "The 20s were a *fabulous* decade for me—very high highs and, at times, very low lows. I remember once in Chile hearing the Frank Sinatra song 'My Way' on the radio and breaking down in wracking sobs. For me that decade held drama, craziness, risk taking, an unshakeable belief in the potential of people to change, and headstrong, in-over-my-head stubbornness. But, my God, was it magnificent."

Stop, Listen, and Be the Best *You* Can Be

MENTOR: Laura Krogh
AGE: 28
I WISH I'D KNOWN AT 26 THAT "you need to believe in yourself and your abilities before anyone else, and to listen to your life and be patient while you try to find your way."

When Laura Krogh appeared on *The Oprah Winfrey Show* discussing the "Turbulent Twenties" in 2001, she had no idea what she wanted to do with her life. Brushing away tears, she told viewers, "I feel lost, trapped. . . . It makes me question my self-worth. Do I not have any abilities? I'm so frustrated. I don't want to be 40 and still unhappy with my life." She says now, "I was stuck in a rut because I wasn't fulfilled, but I didn't know what steps to take to make changes so I'd be happy. I felt hopeless and started to believe that I wouldn't find my calling in life. It made me feel depressed because I just had so much energy and drive to be really great at something, yet I didn't know where to channel my energy. I kept trying new things, hoping that eventually I would find 'it': the thing that would make me happy." But she remained aimless and confused. "I was really trying to make my way in this world and just felt empty and alone. I felt like I was worthless at times and so full of self-doubt. My self-doubt really hindered me because it was almost as though I'd discourage myself and talk myself into believing that I wasn't smart enough or worthy of something better. I felt so many emotions, from frustration and worthlessness to being downright scared of the road ahead if I did or didn't do something different."

Today, the Osakis, Minnesota, native is in a completely different place in her life, with direction and confidence. Laura says the advice that changed her course was something Oprah said to the studio audience during a commercial break: "Stop and listen to your life. Be still and wait. In the meantime, be the best person you can be. Be the best employee, be the best daughter/son, be the best sister/brother, be the best girlfriend/boyfriend. It will come. Be patient. Do things that nourish your inner being." At that moment, Laura says, "I felt like a weight was lifted off my shoulders and I could relax and just do my best at all my roles in life on a daily basis. It was so freeing! It made me realize that perhaps I wouldn't necessarily find all my happiness through finding my passion or my dream job. I started to look around me, saw who I was in the people's lives I touched on a daily basis, and then tried to be the person I wanted to be. Once I let go of the extreme sense of urgency to have everything all at once, I started to figure things out."

Laura started to pay more attention to who she was becoming rather than what she was doing. "I had always felt like I was trying to listen to my life, but I don't think I slowed down enough for that process to happen. I thought if I wasn't busy, then precious time would pass me by. I was always running from one place to the next in search of the next best thing when what I really needed to do was just *stop* and access what was important to me as a person and what I wanted from my life," she says. "It wasn't until my mom was diagnosed with breast cancer that I really stopped. Suddenly my whirlwind of a life halted as I faced the fact that my mom was sick. What was important to me became very clear. I flew home to be with my mom for several weeks while she went to the doctors and had to make serious decisions regarding treatment."

Up until that point, Laura had spent several months working on a feature film as a line producer and unit production manager. But as she helped her mother recuperate, Laura mentally took a step back to analyze whether her career path would mesh with the person she wanted to be. "I had been working my tail off to see my name onscreen for about two seconds. I had always thought it would be my ideal profession and liked the glamorous lifestyle of the showbiz industry. I just never thought it would be so hard with a degree under my belt and living in wonderful, sunny California. I felt guilty sometimes, as though I was being a big baby and whining, but I couldn't help but feel so unsatisfied with my life and as though something major was missing. I realized this path was no longer the path I wanted to go down. I wanted to affect people's lives in another way, and I couldn't do that by making movies," Laura says.

A few months later, Laura went back to school for teaching credentials. Now working as a Spanish teacher, she says she loves her job and her life. "There's nowhere else I would rather be than where I'm at now. The hard work certainly paid off, and now I know I'm where I'm supposed to be. It just feels right. I truly feel I've found my calling and am doing what I'm meant to do on this earth. And though I'm fortunate enough to have found my calling in a job, I still never forget to be the best in my other roles in life because they are equally as important."

Figure Out What Matters Most

MENTOR: John Gonzalez

AGE: 25

I WISH I'D KNOWN AT 23 THAT "you should slow down and think about what's important."

As with Laura, it also took a major shake-up in John Gonzalez's life for him to figure out what he wanted. After he graduated from high school, John decided to take a full-time office job instead of going to college. Though he took a few classes at a community college over the next six years, he mostly spent his time partying with friends. "I had no idea what I wanted to do with my life. I had never given much thought to what I wanted to accomplish, until an incident made me realize what was important to me and required me to stop and *really* think about the direction in which my life was going," John says.

At a party one night, John had a few drinks. He decided he was in good enough condition to drive to a friend's place, where a group of people were going to meet up to go clubbing. He was driving more than one hundred miles per hour on the freeway when he tried to change lanes, jerked the steering wheel, spun across three lanes, and crashed the car into a ditch. "Fortunately, no one was injured, but the experience was an eye-opener. It made me think about the type of life I was leading and the direction it was going. I lived a pretty normal, carefree life for a young man in his early 20s. I had plenty of money because I decided to work full time rather than aggressively pursue a college degree. I had never gotten in any serious trouble, but I had experienced several other close calls that I never really paid much attention to. I guess I had subconsciously fallen into the mindset that I was invincible," John says.

In the days that followed, John spent some time soul-searching. He asked himself questions such as, Who am I? What do I want to do for a living? and What do I want to accomplish in my life? But he didn't come up with an answer until he stumbled across the question, What is important to me? John says, "I found that this is the question that will lead people to realize what they want in life. Some people feel that being successful in their professional lives is most important because it can lead to money or power. Some people believe raising a loving family defines success and focus on that. Others strive to find the balance of being successful at home and at the office. There is no right or wrong answer; the answer lies within ourselves."

For John, the answer lay not in his professional life, but in his lifestyle. "The accident made me realize what was important to me: my family and being able to provide a good life for my family in the future. I've always felt that children should try to surpass the achievements of their parents. Both of my parents have overcome a lot in their lives, worked hard, and were rewarded by being financially stable and raising a good family. I realized this was a stage in my life where I needed to make changes. Making these changes would put me in a better position to be able to surpass the level of success that my parents attained," he says.

For the first time, John started to think about his future. "My income provided a comfortable life for myself, but I realized that when I had my own family, I would be struggling to provide a comfortable life for them unless I had a college degree. So I decided to leave a financially secure job to get a part-time job and finish my college education." John knew he'd be sacrificing a lot, including his spare time and steady income. But it was a change he knew he had to make. "I'm glad I realized the importance of making changes in my life at a fairly young age because it would be a lot more difficult to make these types of changes as I got older."

John moved out of the apartment he rented with a friend so that he would be less likely to be tempted to party rather than study at home. He currently works part time at an office job that is less satisfying than his old one but provides him with the time and money to go to school full time. "I'll be 26 years old when I graduate in 2005, much older than most college graduates but still young enough to begin a new life," John says. "Sometimes change is necessary, even though it can be inconvenient, when we realize that dramatic changes are going to benefit us long term. Making sacrifices we may not want to make is part of growing up. You can also be successful in your own individual way without a preconceived goal in life. As long as you're happy with yourself and the life you're leading, that would make you a success."

Keep Looking

MENTOR: Erik Berkule
AGE: 29
I WISH I'D KNOWN AT 25 THAT "if you know what you're good at, you should explore those things first."

Erik Berkule, a resident of Atlanta, Georgia, isn't entirely sure he knows what he wants, but he does have a plan to find it. "I believe that not knowing what one wants is one of the eternal questions we face. Through the media we're led to believe that all of our hopes and dreams should be self-evident and that it's as easy as waking up in the morning and following your true calling. This is an unfair and untrue assessment of the real state of the world. I'm going on 30, and I have inklings of what I want but still no definite path to that goal," Erik says.

When Erik was a kid, he liked to doodle in class and practiced drawing regularly. During a "boring job" as an insurance company intern in his late teens, he returned to doodling at his desk. "This doodling led me to realize the enjoyment and passion I realize from sitting over a blank piece of paper and creating a new world. I've continued drawing to this day, and I've shown in galleries in San Francisco and Atlanta," Erik says. "Is this what I really want? I have no idea. I enjoy it, but I question it almost every day because oftentimes I have to force myself to the table to draw. There is no handbook for deciding on what you want, and there will rarely be something you'll do all of the time that you know is right. You must try everything that piques your interest, and many times you have to try those things that scare you. I didn't know

I liked displaying my art until I just tried it. I was scared to death to present my first show, but it worked out. Is this the life I want? I don't know, but I will keep looking for it."

More Ways to Conquer

If you are asking, "What if I don't know what I want?" please rest assured that this is not a question you'll be asking yourself for the rest of your life. You *will* find something. Whether you are able to get a glimmer of it from the ideas in this section or the next, or if it takes more time and soul-searching, you are going to stumble over something you want eventually. That is a promise.

The Lotto Question

Set aside some time during which you can be alone in a quiet place, and ask yourself this: "What would I do if I won the lottery and never had to work for a salary again?" How would you spend your time? Shopping? Playing sports? Cooking? Gardening? Exercising? Rearranging rooms? Chances are that many of the activities you enjoy as hobbies can be turned into full-time jobs. The interests I just named, for example, could indicate that you might enjoy a career as a personal shopper or fashion stylist, athletic coach, personal chef, horticulturist or florist, personal trainer, or interior decorator.

It's important to remind yourself that just because it's easiest to get information on the fields of law, medicine, and consulting doesn't mean you even have to consider those careers. Sometimes we forget that there are thousands of jobs out there—entire fields, even—that we've never heard of or imagined. It's the same with lifestyles. People do lead thrilling lives outside of the city and the suburbs. They don't necessarily work in an office or during daylight hours. Just because you haven't been exposed to living in a cabin in the woods or working on a beach in Hawaii doesn't mean that you shouldn't consider it. Furthermore, there are thousands of job ideas that haven't yet crossed your mind. Angelina, for instance, assumes that because she doesn't want to be a vet, there aren't jobs for her that would let her work with animals. But there might be hundreds of options, from marine biologist to groomer to wildlife rehabilitator to animal psychologist to owner of a pet day care center. Your local library most likely has reference books on many of the different career possibilities.

To find other options, it's also helpful to pay attention to everything around you. Let's say you love chocolate (there's a stretch). The chocolate has to be made somewhere, sold by someone, shipped by someplace, placed in boxes designed by someone, marketed by someone, and even taste tested by someone. Behind every product and transaction are long lists of possibilities.

What Do I *Not* Want?

Again, find some time to yourself when you don't have to think about anything else (you could even do this on the subway on your way to work). This time, ask yourself, "What do I *not* want?" Sometimes it's easier to come up with things you know you don't want than to conjure up something you do. Go ahead and list all of the things you can think of that you know you don't want: everything from working in a cubicle to a life of solitude, an apartment in the city to competitive coworkers. Make sure the list is as comprehensive as you can make it. Then flip it. For each item, write down the exact opposite. Don't want to work in a cubicle? Write down that you *do* want an open-air environment, or an office with a door (whichever is more appealing). By the time you flip everything on your list, you may at least see a few ideas begin to emerge.

Ask a Friend

Ask your close friends what they can envision you doing. Don't ask family members, who might somehow have something invested in the life or career you choose (or whom know you so well that they might parrot something you've said before). Simply ask close friends who can offer their objective opinion. Where do they see you? Not what do they want you to do, but where can they plausibly picture you?

Meanwhile, three final tips to help you manage the question, What if I don't know what I want?

• **Not knowing what you want and not knowing how to get there are two different things.** It's possible that somewhere within you, you *do* know what you want. If you know what your passion is, then in a sense you do know what you want; you just don't know how to get it.

• **What you want does not have to be career related.** John's story is especially helpful because he discovered that when he asked himself, "What is important to me?" he wasn't focused on a type of career. His goal was to have a stable, happy family. Could he have it all—a career he loves in addition to a stable family? It's certainly possible. But he made the choice at this point in his life to pursue something that will be the foundation for a stable family in the future. John's story shows us that what you want doesn't have to have anything to do with a job.

• **Take risks.** It's worth repeating Gwen's advice because so many of us are afraid to allow ourselves to take risks. We follow paths that seem familiar because we're scared of the unknown and the uncertain. But if you don't take risks in your 20s, when are you going to? When are you going to grow?

Chapter 2

How do I find my passion?

Larry Yarbrough, 27, has been wrestling with this question since he graduated from college. He says he tried everything, from randomly changing his college major to taking a Myers-Briggs personality test. "I graduated with my degree in sociology only because I figured it would be a great springboard for law. Later I found that law was unfulfilling," Larry says. In an attempt to find his passion, Larry took jobs as a customer advocate for a phone company, hotel clerk, survey interviewer, and patient transporter. "While pursuing the means to a path in life, money has become an issue, so I've decided to get a degree as an x-ray tech. I figure there's a shortage of them now, the curriculum is only two years, and hopefully, helping people will add some intrinsic value to my so-called life."

Larry says he is determined to find a passion because he wants his life to serve some "meaningful purpose." He says, "I've seen others my age making decent money, at least enough to get them a nice wife, car, nightlife, or apartment. It makes me think how all of these material things seem to be so important, yet almost not even worth the trade-off in the time spent working without enjoyment. Through this, I've learned that I personally must be able to experience some sort of internal enjoyment from whatever I may end up doing, no matter how long the journey takes."

But meanwhile, Larry worries that he might not ever find that internal enjoyment. "I've panicked a few times, thinking, 'My God, I'm twentysomething, and I have no direction!' This is why I've had countless nights of tossing and turning, dreaming about being alone and helpless. It makes me depressed and angry at myself."

Nicole Hann, a 30-year-old who will graduate from the University of Colorado at Denver this year, feels similarly panicked. "The question of how to find my passion has plagued me since I was about 13. This is really important to me and is the reason why I look so hard. A lot of people probably think I'm flaky because I have tried so many jobs, had a few majors in college, and have a ton of hobbies. But I'm afraid of settling for something that doesn't completely define and mirror who I am. It seems that if I settle on something, I may be missing out on something else out there," Nicole says. Nicole has studied ballet, attended art school and culinary school, and even tried trapeze. "I've also worked as an artist's model, a social worker, cashier, bank teller, website analyst, chef, and accountant, just to name a few. I'm currently a database administrator finally finishing my bachelor's degree in anthropology. But then what? I've enjoyed all the things I've tried and experienced, but I'm holding out for that one passion. I'm still waiting for something to grab ahold of me, something I can't live without."

Take the "Passion Test"

MENTOR: Geoff Puckman
AGE: 25
I WISH I'D KNOWN AT 20 THAT "what I enjoy now I might not always enjoy, and I should keep an open mind to any possible interest that could develop into a passion."

Geoff Puckman, who graduated from Lehigh University in 2001, has a specific test that he uses to determine what his passions are. He says, "I've found my passions by analyzing what I enjoy. If I come across an activity that I enjoy from time to time, then I consider it just that. But there are times when I find something that I simply can't go without—and that's a passion. The test I use to determine how much something affects me is to see whether I become oblivious to the world when I'm immersed in that activity. At one point, I had an extreme passion for working on cars. I can recall multiple occasions where I was working on a car, and all of a sudden I realized the sun was up and I hadn't been to bed."

Geoff used this same "passion test" to figure out a new direction when, after two years of working in a marketing department of a law firm, he wasn't interested in his job anymore. "As cheesy as it may be, I was looking for a job where I'd wake up in the morning and be excited to go work. In order to have that feeling, I had to find a job that worked with a passion of mine, since the interests and hobbies I'm passionate about consume me that much. So to start my job search, I had to figure out which of my passions I could turn into a job. I settled on the dream of someday having my own restaurant," Geoff says.

Geoff came to define his passion by looking at what activities give him the greatest satisfaction, in *all* areas of his life. "I've always enjoyed entertaining, particularly during parties at school. DJing, mixing drinks—doing whatever is necessary to see that other people have a good time brings me a great deal of happiness," says Geoff, who currently works as a waiter and bartender to build the expertise he'll use when he hopes to open his own restaurant in a few years. "When people at the restaurant come to one of my tables to eat, they're obviously ready for a good dining experience, and my job is to cater to that. I like providing them appropriate service (some are in a rush, some are happy to hang out, others like to converse with the server) and giving them the experience they desire. I get paid according to my level of service, and that works well for both parties. I have a creative side that's more than occupied with creating my future restaurant, whether that entails the physical space, atmosphere, menu items, drink specials, or football parties I might have. I get lost in my ideas about restaurants and bars I plan to open, which fuels my desire to continue in this industry."

Play to Your Strengths

MENTOR: Liz Cleary

AGE: 27

I WISH I'D KNOWN AT 22 THAT "just because you've found your passion doesn't mean that every step of the way you're going to be happy and doing things you're passionate about."

In her early 20s, Liz Cleary, a 1998 graduate of the University of Texas at Austin, was terrified at the thought of figuring out where to work. "My parents had always told me that work should be like play. It's an expression of who you are, your greatest passions, not about paying the bills. But, unfortunately, it had to do that, too. I was cursed with expensive taste and wondered how I could support that by doing something I loved," she says. "I started to think about the things in my life I loved to do that had nothing to do with working. I had never had a job except babysitting and one summer being a camp counselor, but I didn't want to work with kids anymore."

Liz spent more time observing and thinking about the things that made her happy, both as lifestyles and activities. She came up with a list: "I loved people, I loved to travel to new places and observe new cultures, I loved change in scenery, I loved planning events and parties. I was very social and usually preferred to be out with a group rather than spending a quiet night at home. I *loved* clothes. Come to think of it, I had always loved putting visuals together and had read *Vogue* since age seven, when I should have been too young to appreciate it. In fact, any visual magazine, from teen mags to the most artistic avant-garde collector's items, fascinated me. I was really excited in my creative advertising class, looking at visuals and photography. I loved my photography class, but not actually taking the pictures, just when we looked at photos and discussed them. I had spent my childhood shopping for clothes, staring at clothes, making and putting together dolls' outfits, decorating a dollhouse, and playing dress-up. When I was five, I even made a book called *The Glamour and Glitter Book*."

One day, when Liz was reading *Vogue,* she came across an article about fashion shows and realized that it was certain people's jobs to put the shows together—something that sounded fun to her because it combined visual work with people skills. "So the next few years after graduation became about trying all different ends of the fashion industry and imagining the adult lifestyle I wanted. Being an adult had always seemed unbearably dull, so before beginning my internships, I decided to visualize the kind of thirtysomething and fortysomething I wanted to be. Did the people in fashion seem like me? Aside from the visual and creative work I wanted to do in the job itself, what was the lifestyle I wanted? I began to keep a journal and write everything I wanted down after everything I enjoyed doing."

As she progressed through various internships in the fashion industry, Liz met several people who had views and desires similar to the ones on her lists. "They were like me, even down to liking health food and fitness, or at least getting it. They read the books and magazines I read. They saw the plays and exhibits I liked. They went to the clubs I did. They loved to travel and try new things. I just felt at home with these people. I could imagine living like them when I was their age. We shared a similar set of values," she says.

So Liz threw herself into the industry, dabbling in as many parts of the fashion world as she could. She interned at public relations houses, volunteered to set up at fashion shows, interned in the fashion and styling departments at fashion magazines in New York and London, took a sewing class and a jewelry class, and accepted a tough job assisting stylists at a magazine before leaving to work as a freelance assistant stylist. "It wasn't easy. I worked around the clock for some tough people and came home crying a *lot*. I was tired a lot. Some shoots I hated and some I loved. Some involved fashion magazines, some advertising, and some dressing celebrities. I got to compare what I loved and what wasn't worth all the work, and narrow down and define the type of fashion styling I wanted to do," she says. "To relax, I began to make jewelry on the side as a hobby and got a lot of compliments. So I decided to invest the time and money to create an official line. The two careers play off each other and prevent me from getting drained in one area. It's a hard jump from assisting a stylist and fashion editor to doing my own work, and it's hard to launch my own line. But both use the skills that have been interests and passions I've had my whole life."

The excitement and "feeling of being alive" that Liz gets from her work confirms for her that she has found her passion. "Even though it's not easy, when you find your passion, the work itself is easy—still challenging and demanding but easy in a creation way. I'll be on the subway or in the gym and a great idea for a shoot or a new jewelry design comes to mind. I can be up for hours just lost in my work when I'm working on one of my ideas (which isn't 100 percent of my job, but will become more and more as I move up). It's just natural and doesn't feel forced. That's how I know this is a passion, even though it feels like a greater risk," she says. "I'm investing all of my money in my jewelry line, and I have to put my own money into my stylist portfolio. And it's my work, so if someone doesn't like it, it's personal. It is really, really scary, but worth it."

Be Flexible

MENTOR: Jill Cutler

AGE: 27

I WISH I'D KNOWN AT 20 THAT "where you think you're going to be at 20 is probably not where you're going to be at 30. It's just a stepping-stone, and that's a good thing."

In the first *Quarterlife Crisis*, Jill Cutler explained how she thought she had a passion for teaching art but discovered after a while that she didn't like the job so much after all. Because she was so happy in her romantic life and the dance classes she took, she figured she could simply let those carry her through her day job, and she gave up on finding a passion. But that was three years ago.

Because Rob, now Jill's husband, was a naval officer, the couple had to shuffle from base to base. When they were relocated from South Dakota to Washington state, Jill didn't have the state teaching credentials necessary to continue teaching art. "In Washington, I took it as my opportunity to get out of schoolteaching altogether," she says. "Instead, I asked myself to sit back and imagine in what venue I was really happy professionally and found movement to be the answer."

For a while, Jill tried to meld what she believed were her two passions, dancing and working with children, by teaching general dance classes. But while she enjoyed the dancing, Jill felt more like a babysitter than an instructor. "It was fun to break things down to a level children could understand, but I found myself wanting them to be able to grasp more," she says. "I came to believe that while some people are made to work with children, I wanted to teach people who were in my class for the content. So I started to think about teaching adults."

Eventually, Jill stumbled onto Pilates, an ergonomic fitness approach that appealed to Jill because dancers relied on it and because mastering the science involved would challenge Jill and make her feel she "had something more to offer the public." After going through the necessary training, Jill took a pay cut and opened her own small Pilates studio for adults. "I loved teaching adults. After classes they'd approach me and talk to me about things going on in their lives, their health needs, and—something so gratifying to me personally—they'd thank me for the time and energy I gave to them. Kids don't usually approach and thank you for a really great class. While kids just scamper away happy, the actual connection with adults was huge when they'd express how the hour we spent together held such meaning for them. I wanted more," she says.

Hoping to better service her clients, Jill expanded her repertoire by studying every day for more than six months to become certified by the American College of Sports Medicine. "I had to learn a ton of material, but it was totally worth it. I now have the tools to program for all kinds of health concerns, from metabolic to cardiac issues, which means I connect with more people. Since we move so frequently, that my expertise allows people to connect with me is really special to me. It means I start to reestablish myself professionally and socially once we've moved, without a long delay. Plus the fitness industry moves well, so I'm happier sooner, no matter where we go," she says.

Now a personal trainer at a mind-body wellness center in California, Jill is grateful that she was able to wade through a variety of careers to nail down her specific passion. She also knows that while she loves her job now, her passion could fluctuate with time, as it has before. "I don't know if I'll stay in fitness forever, but I do know that I trusted my heart and went with it first," she says. "That led me to figure out where I wanted to be in my career right now. I have complete faith that wherever I'm headed will reveal itself, not because I'm religious but because I'm living proof that it all worked out. I'm happier than ever. And I think it's nice to know that even though you can face a Quarterlife Crisis, you can get through it with faith and hard work, and life can keep on getting better and better even if you had no idea things would go the way they did."

Just Live

MENTOR: Viola Nelson

AGE: 33

I WISH I'D KNOWN AT 25 THAT "passion isn't something you can just manufacture—it's something you have to cultivate, and that takes time and patience."

Viola Nelson, who found her passion in the belly dancing she performs outside of her work in Atlanta, Georgia, says she has a short answer to the question of how to find your passion. "Live.

A passion is something you discover in your lifetime. It's not gift wrapped up in a pretty package, and it's different from something you're just good at doing. A passion is a sacrifice; you may even say you earn it. It may hurt a little, meaning it comes with a price, but a passion is a part of you. There's no sure path to it. You just know you have it," Viola says. "Some people may think their passion is something others won't understand. They may think it's not something you can make a living on. But that doesn't matter. Your passion is what happens in the process of you becoming you. You don't get to live a perfect life. You don't get to always be happy. You don't get to get out of taxes. Life has shit, that's what it is. Your passion is what's in you that's greater than that. It gets stronger with challenge. It's your lifeblood. It's what's in your spirit."

A person can embrace a passion and work it into her personal life completely separate from her professional life, says Viola, who works as a receptionist by day and attends paralegal school at night. "Maybe you will take a trip to Costa Rica and fall in love with the idea of saving the gorillas. Maybe you will find joy in helping children or teaching or writing. Maybe your paintings will brighten up the environment or someone's home. Maybe you find relief in your own personal struggles through an art or some physically challenging sport. Maybe there's this one thing that you want to contribute to the world before you leave it," she says. "If you're in your 20s and haven't found your passion, it's not that you're not passionate. You're just young and haven't been through enough experiences to know your passion yet."

More Ways to Conquer

Find Buried Clues
Geoff's "passion test" is one good way to begin to think about the things that make you happy. Another quirkier method I suggest is to dig up some of the stuff you made or wrote as a small child. It's possible you'll find clues to your identity that got muffled over the

years. The aspirations you talked about and drew pictures of then were your expressions of self before you were aware of society or class-based standards and before peer or family pressure set in.

If your parents didn't keep your childhood things, you can spend some time thinking on your own about what you were like as a child. List the ideas you come up with. I tried this exercise on a 27-year-old on a reality television show. She came up with the following characteristics of herself as a child: she liked to perform in front of people, she was a ham, and she liked speaking different languages. Because her answer to the Lotto Question (see last section—that question is also helpful if you're trying to find your passion) was "travel," she was able to use her answers to come up with an idea she was passionate and excited about: she wanted to host a travel show. This gave her a direction to head toward and a goal to shoot for.

You can also try asking your parents what you wanted to be when you were a kid. (Sometimes this helps; sometimes it doesn't. One white guy I know was asked by a stranger in an elevator when he was 8 what he wanted to be when he grew up. In all seriousness, he answered, "Korean.") The clues aren't always obvious, but they're there. When I recently asked my parents what I wanted to be when I was little, they said I used to say I wanted to be an "astronaut-ballerina-teacher." At first I scoffed: I don't have the stomach for an astronaut, the body for a ballerina, or the patience for a teacher. But then I realized that one aspect of my personality that hasn't changed is that I don't like to focus my career on one single track. So instead of an astronaut-ballerina-teacher, I'm an author-journalist-lecturer. In that sense, I've stayed true to my childhood self.

Tune Out

Another idea to keep in mind is that if you truly want to focus on finding your passion, it's necessary to shed the external noise in your life. Forget what other people think about who you are or what you should do. Weed out from your thoughts the cares and worries about what society thinks. Pay attention only to the directions your self leads you. You need to return temporarily to the mindset you had as a child, before you knew about standards or pressures. You only knew what you wanted. Of all of the ages in your life, this is a time to be relatively selfish because in order to pinpoint your passion, you need to focus on your own happiness above all else.

I also want to echo a sentiment I touched on in the previous section. While some twentysomethings vow that their career will intersect with their passion, your passion doesn't necessarily have to be something you do as a career. It is possible to separate making a living from doing something you're passionate about, and to still be happy. Play the violin in the community orchestra. Save your guided white-water rafting trips for weekends. Do freelance carpentry on the side. It's important to weigh *need* versus *want* when you try to sort out how to incorporate your passion into your life.

Chapter 3

When do I let go of my dream?

In high school in Philadelphia, Tom Evans planned to be a three-sport athlete until he suffered a career-ending injury during football season. When his mother suggested he address his boredom by trying out for the school musical, he did—and fell in love with acting. By the time he graduated, he was the lead in the musicals, had won numerous acting awards, and had found his passion. "Everything crystallized for me. People told me I wasn't going to be able to support myself acting, so I didn't intend to major in theater in college. But once I got there, I realized again how much I enjoyed it," Tom says. Two months after graduating in 1998, Tom began a six-month tour with a national company. "I loved every minute of it, even though life on the road was rough, because I was doing what I wanted to do every day. I learned more in four months there than I did in four years of college."

Following the tour, he moved to New York City, where he appeared in an unpaid opera that performed regularly in the evenings and stacked boxes for a publishing company during the day. After a series of other unpaid performances, Tom was cast with the National Shakespeare Company, with which he toured for eighteen months. He returned to the city when life on the road, away from friends and family, grew to be too taxing. But back in New York, Tom couldn't find work, acting or otherwise, and by July 2001 he was broke. Tired of borrowing from friends and defaulting on his rent, Tom took a part-time job with a sign company that his father worked for. At night he starred in unpaid plays at high-profile venues, in roles like Mercutio in Romeo and Juliet.

Then, just after September 11, 2001, he got what was supposed to be his breakthrough: a well-paid, starring role in a fascinating play about conjoined twins called *Reflections*. Tom was cast as one of the twins. When the play opened, it was so well received that it was scheduled to move to off-Broadway. "But the money got fouled up in the post–September 11th theater depression, and the show didn't open," Tom says. "That's when things went south for me personally. That was my last serious acting gig. If we had gone through and moved uptown, it would have been my big break. I was heavily disappointed, but I didn't realize then how much it would affect me in the long term. I had gone through the stereotypical actor's hardship, but I thought I was there. *Reflections* would have earned me my equity card. When it didn't happen, I didn't know how to deal."

Recently, Tom's boss at the sign company asked him to move into the sales office, a full-time job with a full-time commitment. Tom agreed because he needed the money, and he wanted to prove to his new girlfriend that he could be financially stable. But he finds it difficult to remain focused on his acting now that it's no longer at the center of his life. "I'm not at ease with myself because I know what I want to be doing, and I'm not doing it. What I'm doing is an obstacle to what I want to do. Every once in a while, I think, *That's okay, I'll get back to acting someday*. But, and this might sound overly dramatic and silly, I honestly don't believe I'm being true to what I am if I sell signs for the rest of my life. I don't think that's who I'm supposed to be."

Tom could return to the life of unpaid evening gigs following full days at work but has convinced himself that they are a step down from his capabilities. While he used to be able to leave work at any time to go on auditions, which can last an entire day, he can't do that anymore. He misses auditions for sales conferences, meetings, and everyday job commitments that he can't get out of. His friends at work constantly ask him, "Why are you still here? You're supposed to be an actor." After they saw him in one of his plays, they told him, "We're really holding you back."

Tom's situation is complicated by the fact that he is terrified he is following in his father's footsteps. His father was an artist who gave up his craft at 20 to get married and have children. To earn stability, he went into the sign business. "I think deep down he loves what he has, but part of him misses what could have been. I don't want to end up in the same boat. I love acting. I could sell a million dollars of signs in a day, but I'd still be happier after finishing a good show. I just realized I haven't done an audition in three months—Oh my God, I should kill myself now. At one theater company, I'm known as 'Mr. Shakespeare,' but I sell signs! I have this big gaping hole inside of me. This is all I've ever wanted to be. I don't think I could be the husband and father I could be unless I'm an actor, doing what I want to do," Tom says. "I have two postcards in my room. One says, 'Dreams are made a size too big so you can grow into them,' and the other says, 'Dreams grow old before the dreamer,' and I go back and forth between the two, trying to figure it out."

Risk While You Still Can

MENTOR: Jeff Adams
AGE: 32

I WISH I'D KNOWN AT 25 THAT "you should trust your gut. Not a day goes by that I don't wish I had begun this journey a bit earlier."

In high school, Jeff Adams, a graduate of the University at California, Davis, occasionally enjoyed tinkering on the guitar and piano. One day during his junior year in college, Jeff happened to pick up a friend's guitar and absentmindedly strummed along to a Pearl Jam song playing on the radio. "My friend looked at me like I had sat on his cat, incredulous that I could hear the chords to a song and play them correctly so quickly. It surprised me too. I knew I had stumbled onto something pretty cool, but I wasn't sure what," Jeff says. "I learned to play everything in my CD collection, and soon after that, my friend and I began performing cover songs for the drunken masses at fraternity and sorority parties for free beer. The most exciting part of this new discovery was I found I could create my own songs. The feeling I had after completing my first song was indescribably euphoric. I now knew my purpose in life. The spark had been lit."

The problem was that Jeff had no idea how to pursue a music career. In college he shifted from premed to an English major to a psychology major, even though he didn't intend to enter the field of psychology. After graduation, faced with the prospect of having to earn money to survive, Jeff turned to architecture, another interest he had dabbled in during school. He took an entry-level position with a design firm and remained with the company for nearly a decade. "I've been very happy in my career and make a comfortable living, but all along I felt I was taking the safe route. While I enjoy architecture, music has always been my passion; in my off-hours I continued to write and produce music and had some moderate success doing so. I've always known that, given the opportunity to make a living creating music, I'd jump at the chance. Well, that opportunity is here," he says.

During his ten years at the architecture firm, Jeff continued to pursue a music career on the side. When a song he wrote happened to fall into the lap of a music director for Hallmark Films, Jeff was hired to write several songs for Hallmark's children's animated films. "While I still knew that a career in music was definitely not safe, impractical, and offered inconsistent pay, the spark had become a flame. When not at my day job, I began promoting myself like crazy as a writer, sending CDs to every legitimate record label, producer, and publisher I could locate. And then, just as doubt was settling in, I received a call from one of the largest music publishing companies in Nashville."

The company offered Jeff a chance to collaborate with some of the top writers in country music, and he decided to move to Nashville to give his songwriting a shot. "I have no idea what's going to happen. I'm both excited and anxious. But I know it's a chance I have to take. If I fail, so be it, but I don't want to look back on my life and know I gave up an opportunity to do what I love for a living. The upside is obvious, but there is a downside as well: my salary will reduce dramatically, I'll have to leave my family and friends, and move away from the Bay Area to a foreign city (well, foreign to me, anyway). It is a huge risk at this point in my life. I'll be leaving a career in which I'm happy, successful, and established for one in which I'd essentially be starting over. Initially, I possibly may not make enough money to get by. But I'm going to give it a shot. I have to. Whether I succeed in music or not, I don't want to look back when I'm 73 years old and regret having given up my dream."

Fit Your Dream into Your Life

MENTOR: Steve Grant
AGE: 27
I WISH I'D KNOWN AT 21 THAT "you can still fit your dream into your life, even if it's in a diminished capacity."

Steve Grant, an intellectual property lawyer in Northern Virginia, has always wanted to write a script for a television sitcom. When he was a child, he wrote pretend episodes of *Cheers* and *Golden Girls*. When he was in seventh grade, he won a National Scholastic Art and Writing Award for scriptwriting. Two years later he was watching a pilot for a new sitcom when he realized that the characters were speaking lines eerily similar to lines he had written. "I remember thinking, 'That's what my idea would have turned into.' I felt like I got to see what would happen in that process. At some point I dreamt of having my own show as the head writer, and my name would be at the bottom of the opening credits: 'Created By'—me! Throughout my early 20s as a lawyer, in my head I would sometimes say to myself, 'What if I just went to California,' where I have three degrees of separation to a director I met once. I used to dream of finding him again and presenting my screenplay," Steve says.

But something always held him back. "I'd never actually do it. I think about the risks and the costs, and I don't think I could just quit my job and run off to California and start writing scripts. I wasn't trained. I never took classes. In the office, I'm always told that writing isn't my strong suit. The reality of the business is prohibitive to someone like me just going out there and being successful. It would be very difficult for me to make it work and to make that commitment. I have different priorities than that: stability, the family I hope to have someday, living in this area near my parents. I don't want my dream so badly that I'd be willing to give up what I do now, which I don't hate."

But Steve's certainty that he isn't meant to move to California and work in television doesn't mean that he has let go of his dream. "Even now, as a lawyer working seventy-five hours per week, I will sit down every now and then and write a few lines. I still have free time and 'me' time, so why not? When I'm just sort of sitting and putting words into characters' mouths, it's exciting. My dream isn't to remain a cog in someone else's machine. I want to build my own machine that performs the tasks I want it to perform. But I also need to pay the bills, and boy, are they expensive. So I hold onto my dream and act upon it every now and then. Who knows, maybe after years of five-minute breaks, I'll end up with a great play or something," Steve says. "But that's not my goal anymore. I don't think about my dream negatively; it's not that I lost out on something. I think it's fun to close your eyes and daydream about what that life might have been like. But I'm excited about my life now and being so close to family and friends."

Live in the Now

MENTOR: Emily Stuart
AGE: 25

I WISH I'D KNOWN AT 21 THAT "you're what you want to be, not an assistant/temp/tutor, etc. Work part time and do what you *want* to do. Being scared and doing what you want seems like it's not okay, but it is."

Unlike Steve, who set his Hollywood dreams aside, when we last left Emily in *Quarterlife Crisis,* she was living in Los Angeles and doggedly trying to become a screenwriter. Meanwhile, she made her living tutoring for an educational services company while writing scripts on the side. Since then, Emily has had a few successes: she was hired to write a straight-to-video movie and has had a script optioned, though nothing more has come of it so far. But she hasn't been able to make enough money to give up a non-writing day job.

Now, she says, her dream hasn't changed, but her perspective has. "When I think about how I've grown in the few years from my early 20s to my mid-20s, one thing comes to mind immediately. Price. Simply put, we pay for everything we want in one way or another. Time with our families, a meaningful relationship, money, a career track—these are all things I've watched the people around me trade as we make pressing decisions that affect our futures. And still, everything is about the future. That mindset hasn't changed. Every now and then I make serious mental efforts to make a life that I can enjoy currently instead of one that is based on a fantastic future life. The price of thinking only about the future is extreme because it costs you the present," she says.

Emily says that she often feels that the price she is paying as she chases her desired career is substantial. She points out, "When my class graduated, everyone I knew was clinging to the bottom rung. We were assistants and mailroom gophers; it was tough and felt universally as if it would never end. Three years later most of my friends have been promoted. They have their own desks (maybe even a cubicle), and some have offices and assistants. There are vacations and sick days and dinners out. Houses and cars are bought. As in, actual cars that run and still have that new-car smell.

"I wash dishes and take care of someone else's children. At night, in my closet with a flashlight, I peek at my college degree just to confirm that it really exists," she says. "I've considered giving up, of course. I've thrown tantrums and announced to everyone in the Taco Bell parking lot that this is it; I'm done with writing. I've thrown myself into my job and put all my energy into becoming THE BEST NANNY EVER. Dammit, those shirts will be folded better than at the GAP, and those kids will get to school on time! I've looked into college courses; perhaps I'll get an MFA and teach other people to write. Maybe I'll save the summers for my own scripts. (Right. I never write unless I have to. Contrary to popular belief, writing isn't always fun for writers.) I've considered getting a job in a film studio as a creative executive alongside all the others who planned to be writers, but I'm more comfortable on the other side of the desk."

But Emily has decided that the perks that generally accompany a stable job can have their price as well. "Sometimes they undermine a person who wanted a career in the arts and create a black hole from which it is hard to return. Once a person has car payments and a down payment on the wedding caterer, it becomes much harder to say to loved ones, 'Surprise! I'm going to live on ramen and become a writer after all!' " she says. "As sad and frustrated as I can get as a 'struggling writer' (or 'pre-fame and fortune writer' as I also like to call myself), I know it is nothing to the feeling of killed wishes. I'm not as certain as I used to be that it will work out for me, but I have accepted that this is my craft and I will ride the storm it provides. This is the given. Alongside the writing highs and lows, I put energy into my friends and my wonderful boyfriend. I'm learning to cook really well. I'm finding that climbing the stairs doesn't have to cost me everything. I can create a very fulfilling 'now' life."

There Is More Than One Road to Get There

MENTOR: Eileen McCarthy

AGE: 30

I WISH I'D KNOWN AT 22 THAT "there's not only one right path for you to take."

In her 20s, Eileen McCarthy, a foreign service officer from Seattle, learned to confront her dream not by letting it go but by modifying it. Throughout college, Eileen thought her dream was to be a PhD who did research at a university. "But when I tried it, I was miserable, gained five pounds, and felt like I was pushing a manhole cover with my head," she says. "By chance I took an internship across the country to be close to my boyfriend. I lost the man, but found my career. I realized that what I thought was my dream had been only the way I had defined my dream. What I really loved was interacting with and talking to people of the Middle East, understanding other cultures. I found that I didn't have to be a PhD to do this; I could do it in other ways."

Currently, Eileen, who dropped out of grad school, is posted overseas in a remote Middle Eastern country. "I wouldn't say I gave up on my dream; rather, I had to realize the essential part of what that dream was. So the core of the dream remains, but the original dream has faded. I'm one of the few people I know who loves my job, and I think to get here, it was necessary for me to try my original dream and readjust it. If I hadn't gone to grad school and realized I couldn't spend twelve hours a day in the stacks, I wouldn't be where I am. Sometimes I think about that old dream and mostly laugh at the figure I would have presented and most days feel a sense of relief. But I think we still hold on to those old dreams, and that's okay, too."

As a result of the convoluted path Eileen took to get where she is, she advises twentysomethings who are chasing a dream not to plot out a definite career path before trying something. "Don't try and find the one career," she says. "I know so many friends who try and decide the career before jumping. They end up paralyzed.

Instead, try one, find some parts you like, and then move on. Sometimes you have to jump, and that's okay. It's sort of like the failed relationships I've had. I've learned something from each, and they make the next one better."

More Ways to Conquer

When do you stop pursuing your dream, and when do you go for it? In the past few years, I have spoken to more twentysomethings about this specific question than any other question in this book. It's one of the biggest questions we face, whether we want to start our own business or become a writer, a dancer, or a painter. After hundreds of discussions on this topic, the general consensus leads to this answer: you don't ever have to let go completely, but there comes a point when you have to be realistic and approach your dream differently. And how do you know when it is time to be realistic? You know it's time when your dream is getting in the way of other things that you love.

Before you decide to move on, you may want to make sure that you have pursued your dream the best that you could, so that you'll always know you tried. You could begin by writing down an inventory of the obstacles that stand between you and your dream. Would they be manageable if you tackled them one by one, in small steps? Can you work toward your dream during lunch breaks or off-hours? A friend of mine wrote a novel in increments throughout his time at law school. A couple years after he graduated, the novel was published and became an international bestseller. (Now working on his second novel, he has no plans to become a lawyer.) Another friend started playing the guitar in subway stations after work and now performs frequently in coffeehouses, where he sells his CD.

If your dream is something that's realistic but you can't surmount all of those obstacles *yet,* there's no reason you have to change a dream simply because you can't get it *now.* Instead, it's something to work toward and a motivation to inspire you. Have you given it your all? If you have, and haven't made the slightest iota of progress, you might be going at it the wrong way. And if you have been pursuing your dream fruitlessly for years and now find that to continue to pursue it in precisely that way you have to sacrifice too many other good things in your life, then yes, it's probably time to reevaluate your methods.

But reevaluating your dream doesn't equate to giving it up. Here are four steps to go about the task of modifying your dream without letting go of it:

Dissect Your Dream

Let's say you dream of becoming an actor. You might be convinced that you won't be fulfilling your dream unless you land a full-time acting role on Broadway or in Hollywood. When you're ready to move into the next phase, you could dissect your dream by analyzing which parts of the dream you truly need. Is it the actual acting—the inhabiting of other characters and personalities? The rush of performing in front of other people? Or would you never be satisfied unless you achieved the rank of superstardom?

Gauge What's Realistic

After you've dissected your dream and isolated the part of it that you believe you truly need, it's a good time to work out which aspects of it are realistic versus those that are likely unattainable at this point in your life. This process requires as much objectivity as you can muster and can be a difficult step to work through. If you have credit card debt out the wazoo because you can't support yourself while pursuing an aspect of your dream full time, it's not realistic to think you could continue pursuing it in the same way at this time.

Let Your Heart Soar but Keep Your Head Grounded

Once you have figured out which parts of your dream *are* realistic for now, you can either pursue them full time or chase them part time while working on something else on a parallel track. If your dream doesn't pay the bills, do what you need to do to pay the bills and pursue your dream when you're not at work. It's not all or nothing. You can always, *always* pursue parts of your dream on a smaller, modified scale. If the dream is too far fetched, modify it. Can't be a movie star? Join a local theater troupe or teach acting classes. Can't write for the *New York Times*? Write for a small local paper. You never know where the connections will ultimately lead you; in fact, you could end up on a track that ends up plunking you right where you wanted to be.

As Wanda Lessing, a 28-year-old lawyer, says, "You should never let go of a dream, but it's important to realize that you have to get a job and pay bills, and that's just reality. Somewhere along the line you have to figure out that your dream may not come in the form of your full-time job." Wanda says her work is interesting but unfulfilling. But during her off-hours, she has become heavily involved in her community and in local politics. Last year she was unanimously nominated to run as a candidate for probate judge in her hometown. "Granted, I lost, but I had a good showing, and I found something I'm passionate about: politics and giving back," she says. "I'm still very involved in politics, and I have a lot of fun with it. And, hopefully, at some point in my life, my 'hobby' and my 'career' will intersect."

Consider Other Options

Here's another thought. If you haven't yet been able to achieve your dream, how do you know it's precisely the right path for you? You won't know, of course, until you get there or are on your way. Keeping this in mind, you should remain open to the idea that there may be other ways to get at your dream and other, less obvious paths that might be even more suitable for you and relevant to your passions. That's what happened to Eileen, who realized on her way to a PhD that it wasn't the PhD that she actually wanted. It's important to keep an open mind that there might be other identities possible for you that you'll love, even if they're not exactly the picture you've been carrying of yourself.

Don't Lose Yourself in Your Future

Lastly, a common cause of the Quarterlife Crisis is that we get so caught up in what our lives will be like several years down the road that we forget about enjoying the present. So to reiterate Emily's advice, make sure you are still living *in* the present, rather than *for* an uncertain future.

Chapter 4

What if I don't get what I want by the age I thought I'd get it?

For many of us, the Quarterlife Crisis is a result of feeling that we're falling behind in some aspect of life, whether in work or relationships. Sara Bauleke, a 1999 graduate of Occidental College, says she has an ongoing struggle with the issues of age and achievement. "When I was young, 27 seemed *really* old. Now that it's a few months away, I'm starting to feel old—not because 27 is old, but because in my mind my life was to be more established than it actually is. My mother had her first child at 27, which is why the age has such significance to me. That always seemed like a good age for kids, I thought. So being unmarried and childless at 27 isn't where I wanted to be in life."

To a casual observer, Sara has an enviable life: good friends, fun jobs in exciting cities, and a newly minted master's degree. "But sometimes I find myself depressed that I've deviated from 'The Schedule,' though I know that I am devaluing the life experiences I've had. Everyone lives at their own pace, but it's difficult to accept that mine is different than what I anticipated it would be."

Heather Watson, a Washington State University graduate from Issaquah, Washington, has just turned 30, a birthday she struggled with. All of the thirtysomething women she knows have told her that the 30s are their best years yet, but somehow, Heather can't stop thinking about the goals she had expected to achieve by now. "Of course, I'm looking forward to all that my 30s will entail, but there is so much I thought I would have already done and so many facets of my life that I thought would already be in place. I know I'm still young by most people's standards, but at times there's almost a sense of panic when I take a serious look at my future, though there's also a sense of excitement for all that lies ahead. There's so much I have yet to accomplish and do."

Heather has also wrestled with the notion that by 30 she should be in a different career, because once she gets into her 40s, she says it will be too late to make a career change. "I have a good job I'm good at, but I know deep down in my heart this is not what I am meant to do. I think I know what I should be doing, but pushing forward and doing it is easier said than done. At 30, I feel as though this is the time to make the change. I can't enter a new career ten years from now when I'm 40. Or can I?"

Sometimes Timelines Can Help

MENTOR: Nicole Hann
AGE: 30
I WISH I'D KNOWN AT 28 THAT "there's not as big of a rush as you think. A lot can happen in two years, and it will all work out eventually."

When Nicole Hann turned 28, she began to panic about all the things she had planned to accomplish by the age of 30 but hadn't yet achieved. "My 20s were full of anxiety, fun, turmoil, excitement, fear, love, hate—you know, all the teenage stuff but somehow more scary and real. I feel like I sort of clawed and stumbled (and sometimes staggered) my way to 30," she says. "But at 28 I began to freak out a little when the sudden realization struck that I was nearing 30 and hadn't yet graduated from college, I had absolutely no equity, and marriage looked to be in the very distant future. That frightened me. Everyone wants to be in a certain place by certain ages in their life. So I went back to school, first of all, and concentrated on graduating, at the very least. The rest I just got lucky with (okay, and very pushy with my now fiancé)."

For Nicole, the impending "deadline" of 30 spurred her into action. But though she managed to squeeze into two years what she had wished to gain by 30, she says she won't try to hold herself to a timeline again. "The only thing you can do is try to focus on your goals and be as patient as possible," she suggests. "The most important thing to do is to *not* settle on anything or anyone just because you're trying to meet a deadline. People have accomplished their goals later in life than they would have hoped and have been happy. On the other hand, people have settled for things so that everything fits into their timeline and have become quite unhappy. A timeline is a good guideline, but don't make it the rule at the expense of long-term happiness. It's not that important! Hold out for what you *really* want."

Deadlines Can Be Adjusted

MENTOR: Catalina Bumatay
AGE: 33
I WISH I'D KNOWN AT 30 THAT "there's no such thing as control of your life. Life just happens."

Catalina Bumatay, a lifelong resident of San Francisco, used to think that if she didn't get what she wanted by a certain age, she was "doomed for failure." By the time she turned 30, for example, she fully expected that she would be making more than $30,000 a year. "Ha! What a joke. I was working as a receptionist making $26,000 a year. Then I also had the belief that I should have the house, car, and kids by the time I was 30. I didn't have any of those things. I really beat myself up for it, too. The funny thing is I don't know where the thinking came from; I just know that this thinking haunted me almost all of my adult life," she says.

A self-proclaimed "party girl" in high school, Catalina chose not to take the SATs and ended up going to community college for a few years while working part time. At 21, Catalina had to drop out of school and work full time because of credit card debt and an illness in the family. She hopped from job to job, including stints at Baskin-Robbins, Track n Trail, Tower Records, Casa de Fruita, Jay Jacobs, Pacific Bell, FoodsCo, Neiman Marcus, and Niketown. Eventually, Catalina landed a corporate concierge position at a consulting company, a job she kept for two years.

"By then I had had enough time to figure out what I wanted to be when I grew up," she says. "Also, my 30th birthday was pending, and I was feeling a little bit behind in comparison to my friends and cousins. I kept hearing my mother saying, 'When I was your age, I had two children, a house, a car, and a good job.' But when I finally met my significant other, he told me, 'It's not what you acquire by a certain age; it's how you acquire it and if it makes you feel satisfied.' I realized that while I was worried about getting this and that, life was happening right before my eyes. So I have finally gotten rid of that god-awful thought that I have to get things done by a specific age."

Catalina says she would tell people caught in the crush of self-imposed deadlines that they need to forget them. "Relax; things happen for a reason. Life happens. There's no more to it than that. I always hear in my mind, and I think people should ask themselves, 'Who are you racing? And what are you trying to prove?' "

Take Action, but Be Realistic

MENTOR: Angela Netherland McBride
AGE: 26
I WISH I'D KNOWN AT 22 THAT "my worth doesn't depend on my professional success; there are so many more important things. I just want to grab the me I was then and tell her to lighten up and enjoy life."

"If I look back at where I thought I'd be at 26, it's a lot different from where I am," says Angela Netherland McBride, who is from Columbus, Ohio. "I'm supposed to be a single workaholic making $15,000 more a year than I do now and living in a different part of the country. In reality, I'm married to a great man, building a huge portfolio in a nonprofit organization, and stuck in the Midwest. But I'm probably happier now than I ever thought possible. I'm beginning to think that no one should ever write out those ridiculous five- or ten-year plans. They only set us up for failure and disappointment."

Angela recommends three steps for twentysomethings worried about their future timeline:

Trace your timeline. "Ask yourself these questions and think hard about the answers: How did you come up with the timeline for your life? Was it realistic in the first place? Did you actually set these goals, or are they coming from someone else?"

Keep goals in perspective. "Look at your goals and timeline again. There are bound to be some accomplishments that you expected by now but didn't achieve, and you're probably still doing okay."

Take pride in your progress. "Now look at all the things you did accomplish that weren't on the list. Don't limit it to career or relationship goals. Learning to like yourself is just as important as career achievement, but no one thinks to write that up in a plan."

More Ways to Conquer

If you think about it, it's natural that our generation has a tendency to attempt to schedule our lives. Compartmentalizing our lives into rigid, timed schedules is a logical progression stemming from childhood days heavily regimented by school and activities like piano lessons, playdates, and soccer games. We've been brought up to emphasize time-management strategies, from our busy childhoods to the high school days when many of us frantically tried to cram as much college-application fodder into our lives as we could without collapsing. It's not much of a stretch to go from day planners to life planners. But the problem with trying to hold ourselves to rigid life deadlines is that if we don't make the deadlines, we feel as if we failed. And there's no reason we should feel that way.

Having goals is fine. Planning for things that are more than you think you deserve or are slightly out of reach is also fine; aiming high is how we motivate ourselves to do better. But trying to pin deadlines on aspects of your life that you can't control is not fine; it's unfair to yourself. It may be helpful to try the following exercise:

Deconstruct Your Timeline

Divide a piece of paper into two columns: "Goals I can control" and "Goals that rely on other people." Want to run in a marathon? Put that in the first column. Want to marry by 30? Put that in the second. Then look at each item in the second column and rate it "highly contingent" or "somewhat contingent" on other people. Seeing these goals written down should provide a more balanced, relaxed view that could help you realize what you can't control. It may also help you to prioritize trade-offs, such as "This job is in a better location, but if I take it, I might not meet my career goals."

The feeling that you have to achieve a lot by age 25 to be a success is a new one. Members of our generation have higher, usually more unrealistic expectations of ourselves than had previous generations. You need to take it easy on yourself. If you look around, you'll likely find that the toughest pressure to succeed is coming from you. Therefore, you have control over the clock that's running your life. Ease it up. There is no reason you need to nail down the various aspects of your life—home, job, social circle, romantic partner—by age 25 or 30. Regularly remind yourself that there is no rush to decipher your identity in your 20s. You have the rest of your life for that.

After speaking to thousands of twentysomethings in the past few years, I've found that the people who get through their

Quarterlife Crisis quickly and relatively painlessly all have one thing in common: their attitude. They haven't placed some matrix of age-related deadlines over their lives. Instead, they view their 20s like a journey. These are the people who, instead of saying, "I'm going to be a lawyer by the time I'm 26," will take a step back from their lives, maybe to work in another country or take a nonchallenging job while they think things through, really just taking some time off from the fast-track path that too many of us are intent on catapulting toward immediately after school. These are the people who understand that there's no rush.

If you have a timeline that encompasses more than the standard five- to ten-year career plan, or if somewhere along the way you decided that you needed to acquire the complete boxed set of spouse-career-home by the time you hit a certain age, you need to ask yourself what the rush is. Where did you get the idea that you must hurry up and choose something simply so you can get ahead? You need to add a new voice inside your head, one that says, "So what?" What if you don't get married by 30? So what? What if you haven't paid off your loans or debt by 35? So what? What if you're not a stand-out success by 28? So what? If you were to achieve everything you wanted in life by the age of 30, then what would you do for the next fifty years? You have time. You don't have to get to everything right now.

Chapter 5

How do I start over? or, What if I spent
years working hard and now realize I made
a mistake?

Rachel Jessup, a 24-year-old from Detroit, spent four
years in college studying the field of sports management. Everything she did in school was directed toward the career she expected to have in that field. She worked hard for the opportunity
to get a foot in the door and was rewarded with a job after graduation working for a professional sports league. "The first year was
great, the second year I started taking initiative, and now my third
year has been like 'Oh. *This* is what I do.' And I've been thinking,
'Did I make a mistake?' It's a scary moment, and it's overwhelming
to think about," she says. "This is a tough field to get into, so what
if I do make a change and don't like it, and want to come back?"

Rachel's questions have had a "ripple effect": her sister just
moved out of her apartment, her friends are in serious relationships that leave less time for her, and she finds New York City to
be too much sometimes. "I've thought of leaving the city, not
having anything keeping me here. I have this desire to break out,
but I'd be starting over from scratch if I went somewhere else.
I'm going to be 25, and it's easier to make friends in a new place
right out of school when everyone else is in the same boat. But I
think to myself, 'What am I doing here? Why am I working

here? Is something wrong with me?' I pelt myself with these questions all the time, but I have this fear of starting over again. What am I going to do?"

Prioritize Happiness over the Past

MENTOR: Mark Anestis
AGE: 28
I WISH I'D KNOWN AT 24 THAT "I should take the leap of faith and not worry so much about the decision."

Two years into medical school at the University of Connecticut, Mark Anestis realized he hated what he was doing. "I found myself waking up each morning at the crack of dawn dreading the grueling hours ahead. On my way to the health center each day, I'd wonder why I spent so much time and effort over the past six years putting myself into this horrible position. Looking back, I'd say it wasn't a total loss. I really enjoyed learning about how the body works and what can go wrong. But the practice of medicine itself was brutal. There was so much bureaucracy to deal with—paperwork and insurance—it drove me nuts," Mark says.

After months of agonizing how to start over when he had invested so much time and energy in this particular path, Mark decided to leave school. Immediately he was inundated with naysayers. " 'You're less than two years away from your MD,' they said. 'Stick it out. You've done all this work; don't give it up for nothing.' Or, 'You're just going through a phase.' " Mark says, "Instead of saying I was 'dropping out' of medical school, I made it less formal. I told people I was 'taking a break' to think things over, even though deep down I knew it was forever."

Four months after he left medical school, Mark began his new job search in earnest. He contacted the founder of a local tutoring company, and once he started tutoring, he learned he loved it. "I realized that working with high school students would allow me to help younger people through the difficult college-application process, which appealed to me because I liked teaching and I liked working with people," Mark says. "In late 1999, the tutoring profession wasn't the booming industry it is now. It was the sort of thing where when someone asked me what I was doing for work, I'd reply, 'I'm tutoring,' only to hear, 'Oh, that's nice. What are you doing to make money, though?' People couldn't believe I could somehow support myself by tutoring."

The first year was slow as Mark tried to build a client base. But by the end of the second year, he had enough clients and revenue to open an office. Today he runs a successful, expanding business that provides tutoring and prepares test-prep materials. When he recalls his years of hard work to get into and then to survive medical school, Mark often wonders, "How the heck did I get myself into that medical school mess?" He says, "I think the most important thing about how I cope with the years of medical school in my past is I don't look back at those years as time wasted. No way I would have written and published an AP biology book had I not learned as much as I did in the first two years of medical school. I don't look at medical school as a mistake as much as I look at it as an important part of my development into where I am now as a person."

To twentysomethings who think they are in the predicament of realizing that they have spent years working hard on something that was a mistake, Mark says it's important to push yourself to embrace change before you dig yourself any deeper. "The bottom line is you're not alone if you find yourself waking up every day thinking, 'Ugh, why am I doing this? This is awful.' Not a great feeling to have. Don't let yourself accept it as an okay thing that will pass and get better. You can't do something on a daily basis that you dread. I was lucky I had people who stood behind me and supported my decision. It made it easier for me to be strong and to say out loud, 'I've somehow gotten myself on a career path that doesn't make me happy, and I want off.' It was one of the hardest choices of my life and one of the best things I have ever done. I'm happier now than I've ever been," Mark says. "Don't let inertia carry you into that position where you find yourself wishing you had made a change way back when. If you feel that you need to make a change, make that change, have faith, and hope for the best. Even if the first thing you try after the change isn't perfect, it doesn't mean you've made a bad choice; it just means you have to keep looking. Yes, it's a huge decision to bust out of medical school or deviate from your career path, but happiness and sanity are so much more important than career certainty. This isn't something I could have known without having taken the leap and found out what it felt like to do so."

Reshaping Your Life Can Be a Gift

MENTOR: Cara Briskman
AGE: 37
I WISH I'D KNOWN AT 25 THAT "nothing is irreversible except death. Our decisions, commitments, and directions can be changed at any time."

When Cara Briskman was in her 20s, she lived in her hometown of Scottsdale, Arizona, near her parents and best friends. She met the "perfect" husband and was able to stop working. She was happy. Then her husband left her. She says, "I was faced with some choices: to stay and figure out how to rebuild my life in Arizona or to build a new life someplace else. That kind of opportunity comes along sometimes never in a lifetime, to pick up and leave all that's safe, all that you know, and take off for the unknown. I went for it."

In 2000, Cara moved to Vashon Island, a tiny island near Seattle. She made a deal with her sister, who was living there and building a house, to live on her property for six months: she would live in a yurt (a tentlike structure of wood and canvas) erected on the property while her sister was mostly out of town for work. In return for helping to work on the house, Cara could live rent free while she figured out her life. "Am I going to live on the island? Am I going to go back to school and live in Seattle? Am I going to work? What am I going to do?" Cara asked herself repeatedly.

Cara had gone from an 1,800-square-foot house in Scottsdale to a twelve-foot-diameter tent. She had a wood stove for warmth and a Coleman two-burner propane cooktop for cooking. Her bathroom was an adjacent deck with a toilet, sink, and aging clawfoot tub that had been rigged with a shower that was heated by propane. "I went from seventy-degree weather to showering outside in thirty-two degrees and rain," she says. "But the space was beautiful. It was homey and warm and filled with my favorite things. Everything else was in storage waiting for me to decompress and figure it out. The yurt was situated on five acres of forest that were beautiful and invigorating. I had the time and the space to decide what I wanted: what I wanted to be, what I wanted to do with my life, and I mean in every way. What was the essence of me going to be? What was my foundation going to be? I was a wife, I was a manager, I was a student, I was someone's sister, daughter, friend. Now who was I going to be? I was handed the chance to reshape my life."

To create her new life, Cara broke down the aspects of her current one. "I looked at the things I was good at, the things I was terrible at, and the things I wanted to learn and experience." Then she acted upon that analysis. Within six months of her move to Vashon Island, Cara had a new home (a cottage she bought), job (a commercial embroidery business she started out of her home), great friends (including a new boyfriend), and renewed sense of self. She was "recharged," she says, and at peace with both the life she had left and the new life she had just begun. "As far as starting over again, it is without a doubt the scariest thing a person can do, at whatever age, whatever place you are, be it a job, a home, or a lifestyle you are leaving. But you have the power to embrace the change, embrace the new, and truly be who and what you want to be. It sounds so trite, but the truth is, the first step to starting over is ending something. Courage and faith in yourself are the key ingredients."

Life Is Constant Readjustment

MENTOR: Jason Crispin

AGE: 25

I WISH I'D KNOWN AT 23 THAT "it's okay that you don't know everything; you still have a lot of learning and growing ahead of you. And it's never to late to start again."

When Jason Crispin, an Ocean County College student from Toms River, New Jersey, was in his early 20s, he was dating a girl he met in high school and working toward a career in the culinary arts. But soon after his marriage, Jason began to suspect it was time for a change in several areas of his life. "The marriage got off to a terrible start, and it didn't take long for us to stop talking to each other. We both knew right away that we had made a mistake. She spent more time with her friends than with me, and I began to start drinking very heavily. She moved out after eight weeks of marriage. After she left, I fell into a very deep depression and was drinking every day. I went on living that way for the next sixteen to eighteen months, getting worse and worse."

At 23, Jason decided he needed "to change and change fast." After the failure of his marriage and the realization that his work was becoming increasingly less gratifying, Jason vowed to start over by completely overhauling everything he didn't like about himself, including his job, health, education, and his outlook on life. "Starting over for me was so hard. I knew I had to stop drinking first or I'd never be able to change anything about myself. Next I had to figure out what I wanted to change and in what order. I wrote it all down item by item and looked at it every day to measure my progress. It was important to know that change doesn't come overnight; it comes with time, so I had to have patience."

At the top of Jason's list was to go back to college and get his degree. "Next, I had to change the way I looked at everything. When I was depressed, I never saw the good side of anything, even after I stopped drinking. I started to develop a new way of thinking. The idea behind it was simple: Do what's best for Jason. I had to make *me* happy; I had to do what was best for me, in every situation. And I had to get back into shape because I had put on thirty pounds since I got married," Jason says. "Now, every time I cross off an item on the list, I add another item on, always growing and changing. I have fears and nervousness all the time, but change for me is exciting, and I know it will make me a better person in the end. My advice to twentysomethings would be, don't be afraid to change, but you have to want to change in order for it to work, and you have to work toward it every day. To start over, all you have to do is get the courage to change, figure out exactly what you want to change, write it down, put the list where you can see it every day, and go for it, and don't stop till you change. The trick is you have to really want it. It only works if you want to change bad enough."

More Ways to Conquer

You should never base the rest of your life on decisions you made when you were young. When you chose your post–high school education (or whether to continue it) or when you chose your major, you were young. How can you know at 17 or 18 what you want to do for the rest of your life? It's unreasonable to hold yourself to a decision you made before you knew who you really were. As Mark told me, "Don't let yourself do something simply because you've started on a path and feel that you *should* complete it. Life is too short for that."

Another idea to remember is that nothing is a waste if you learned something from it. Learning what you're not cut out for counts. Moreover, your past experiences did more than merely lead you toward a goal that you may have decided you don't want anymore. Whatever you did in the past led you to where you are and who you are today. Your background has honed your strengths, exposed weaknesses, revealed likes and dislikes, broadened horizons, and refined skills. Simply because your goal has changed doesn't mean you won't be able to use the lessons your past experience has given you.

Cara offers a quick checklist to help determine whether to start over. She says, "If you aren't finding happiness, if you're spending more time complaining than being excited, if you're thinking more about how unhappy you are with your job or your partner than you are about what tomorrow might bring, then do not be afraid to start over." It takes courage and strength to start over, absolutely. But if starting over is something you're hesitating about although you know you need to do it, ask yourself, "What am I afraid of? Is that realistic? Is it likely? And is that situation worse than the situation now?" No matter how much you have to overcome, it will be worth it by the time you can look back from a better place.

The mentors' answers all come down to one bottom line that is perhaps the best guide for this question: It's better to make a change now than to keep living your mistake simply because you worked hard to get there.

Part 2

Relationships

Finding love, or at least finding someone to connect with, ranks either first or second on most twentysomethings' priority lists (the competing priority is finding a sustainable career). This is not to say that all twentysomethings are anxiously scanning the horizon for a mate; in fact, perhaps too little is made of young adults who are single and happy, and content to remain that way. But generally, at some point in our 20s, many of us begin to get anxious about finding the person with whom we'd like to spend our lives and fall into a Quarterlife Crisis because of it.

One of our difficulties with romantic issues is that this is an area of life over which we can't have total control; it is, of course, contingent on other people's feelings. And yet we often do everything we can to try to assert control, whether we're trying to meet someone, shift our feelings toward that person, shift that person's feelings toward us, or fit that person into the mold we want him or her to fit. We crave serendipity, but at the same time, many of us try to put ourselves out there as much as possible to increase our chances of encountering it, which seems beside the point.

Some of us try so hard that dating has become as much of a time and energy sucker as a part-time job. It has become tough to find classy ways to meet new people without seeming desperate or sleazy. Dating as a twentysomething is a lot of work, and especially while we're trying to juggle the other overwhelming aspects of our lives, it can be difficult to make time for it. Finding romance has almost become a chore instead of the fun, exciting exploration it's supposed to be.

But meanwhile, the twentysomething dating we see on television gives us the impression that we're not doing it right. Sometimes it seems like the easiest way to meet a date is to get on a reality TV show. When our resources are shows like *The Bachelor,* we're still left wondering how we're supposed to meet twenty-five decent dating candidates in a year, let alone a night. In the new social background we enter as twentysomethings, we flounder in a limbo somewhere between college hookups and adult dating, in a Quarterlife Crisis centered on the difference between expectations and reality (of the nontelevision variety). In this section, you won't find "rules" to follow or silly guarantees. But you will find insightful answers to questions the usual dating guides don't address—answers that might give you some new ideas or perhaps the courage and confidence you need to try a different approach.

Chapter 6

Why am I having trouble meeting people?

"Where in the hell are all of the single, professional, twentysomething men?" asks Aimee Lerner, a 26-year-old in Harrisonburg, Virginia. "There's a *Sex and the City* quote that sums this question up well for me: 'It's like the riddle of the Sphinx. . . . Why are there so many great unmarried women and no great unmarried men?' Amen! I'm not a hermit. I go out to bars, art shows, coffeehouses, but I can't seem to find anyone who's even a little bit compatible with me. Almost everybody I work with is married, and they keep telling me that it's not me; it's the area we live in. But how long can I realistically believe that I'm not at least partly to blame?"

Mark Gomez, a 25-year-old in Dallas, says he has made more close friends in his mid-20s than at any other time in his life, but wonders if the security of that tight group is preventing him from meeting possible dates. "I guess we're close because we're all single, and who else are we going to be around with? It's great having good friends, but at times when I'm hanging out with my friends, I get scared by the fact that I feel very comfortable with how things are. I think to myself, *Why am I always with the same people? I should be out somewhere with some girl.* I can't keep doing this or else I'll be single for the rest of my life!" he says. "So I set up a plan to go to social events and meet as many people as possible with the hopes that somewhere I'll meet someone I can date. I do this for a while and then get frustrated because I can never find that girl who will blow me away. And then I think to myself, *Wait, why am I with these new people? I already have good friends.*"

Stay in the Game

MENTOR: Dan Schwartz
AGE: 27

I WISH I'D KNOWN AT 24 THAT "there was at least one person out there who would really like me exactly as I am. If I'd known that, I wouldn't have stressed so much about being the person I was."

In the first *Quarterlife Crisis* book, Dan Schwartz struggled with this very issue. When I interviewed him for that book, he told me that he was anxious about finding someone with whom he could start a family. At that point in his life, he had decided to make "an extra effort to find the right woman." Because he disliked looking for dates in bars or clubs, where the atmosphere was too loud to have a conversation, he tried joining groups, such as an a capella music group and a recreational comedy troupe, but he didn't meet the "right" woman there. Instead, he dated a few women he met at parties and one who worked at his company, but none of them panned out for the long term.

When I checked back in with him for this book, Dan's luck in the romance department had completely turned around. "The truth is, the problem isn't that you can't meet people. You meet people all the time. It's just that you don't connect with people. I wasn't really connecting with anybody who I knew I wanted to be with," Dan says. Not long after I interviewed him that first time, Dan went to a Fourth of July party thrown by someone he knew from work; it was a low-key affair on a roof deck overlooking a river where there were fireworks. As Dan walked in, a girl on her way out stopped to say goodbye to the host.

Dan was instantly attracted to the girl. When she asked the host for directions, Dan jumped in to help. "We started talking, and I found out she had read about the party on a Jewish group list and came even though she didn't know a single person there. She brought homemade Rice Krispies treats, which I thought was cute," Dan says. "We connected immediately and found quickly that we had a few major things in common. We talked for twenty minutes, and then she gave me her number. I still have that piece of paper in a safe-deposit box to give to our future kids and grandkids. After eight months we got engaged, and now we've been married for a year and a half."

Looking back, Dan is glad he met his wife at a time when he was open minded but not allowing himself to be desperate. "I had the right attitude. I was ready for love, so I was open to it. At the same time, I didn't lower my standards. A couple weeks before I met my wife, I went on a first date with another woman. She was nice, but we didn't click, and we ended it there. Good thing; otherwise I might not have asked my wife out when I did," he says.

In response to Aimee's question about where the men are, Dan promises that they are out there. "There are a lot at my business school!" he says. "Seriously, they're around. But I've noticed that single professional women want single professional men, while single professional men are open to anybody." Dan has several words of advice for twentysomethings who are having trouble finding people to connect with:

Get out of the house. "You need to think about places where you could potentially meet people. It doesn't have to be a lot of people because, really, you only need to find one. You need to put yourself out there."

Do things that are comfortable for you. "If I had tried the bar scene, I would have failed miserably because that's not what I am."

Lead with your strengths. "If your strength is staying at home and reading books, that's probably not going to get you a date. But you could use this interest to join a book club."

Be creative. "Make an effort. *Queer Eye for the Straight Guy* is all about putting thought and creativity into things, which is the same idea here. Dating is about making good impressions."

Be authentic. "It was important not to misrepresent myself too much. I tried to be straightforward about my beliefs. For example, on our first date I ordered a cheeseburger even though she kept kosher. We had a long conversation about keeping kosher, and I wanted to be straightforward that I liked cheeseburgers. I didn't want to keep anything below the surface that could lead to a conflict down the road."

Be Open to New Opportunities

MENTOR: Wanda Lessing

AGE: 28

I WISH I'D KNOWN AT 25 THAT "you shouldn't be afraid to get the word out that you're on the market."

A few years ago, after Wanda Lessing had gone on several first dates that she decided would not proceed to second dates, she stopped actively looking for a boyfriend and swore off all set-up attempts by her friends. "I used to feel like if I didn't go out on a Friday night, then I was missing the opportunity to meet the man of my dreams. After starting work and being tired on Fridays, I gave up on that theory," Wanda says. "I decided to have him come find me and just live day to day and have fun. I stopped worrying about getting married by 30 and instead focused on a goal I could work toward, like buying a house."

One Friday night, Wanda's sister and brother-in-law convinced her to go on a blind double date with them and "a mystery man." She says, "I so didn't want to go because I really didn't trust their judgment. But he turned out to be my now boyfriend, and after a year together, I think we'll be together forever. After years and years of bars and parties and dates, I met my boyfriend on a blind date. Who knew?"

Wanda now has several suggestions for twentysomethings who wonder where to meet people. "You meet people all the time, but you just have to keep your eyes open. Talk to everyone," she says. "Get out there and live your life. Do the things you love. Go out to bars if you like. Listen to people. Also, you may be looking for the 'perfect person' to fit your idea of the 'perfect' life. This is just a recipe for disaster. If you feel like staying home one night, stay home. Also, stick with it. It only takes one right person to make the difference."

Relax

MENTOR: Devon Linden

AGE: 27

I WISH I'D KNOWN AT 23 THAT "I should chill out. The more you focus on things that interest you instead of searching for people, the more you're going to hone in on what you're meant to have."

Devon Linden, another twentysomething from the first *Quarterlife Crisis,* mentioned back then that it was difficult to meet people outside of work, where her fellow teachers were older and mostly married. Now she explains, "When I graduated college and started teaching right away, the whole relationship thing was tough. What's a nice single girl to do, right? Well, I decided to try the personals. Oh, come on, we've all perused the personals before, you know, trying to decide which ones are for real. Well, I started looking a bit closer and even circled the ones that intrigued me, and then I did it: I found the balls to actually call one. We spoke for a bit but realized it wasn't a romantic connection. Then I thought, 'Wait a minute. I have to pay to make these phone calls, but I can place an ad for free.' So I found my even bigger balls and did it."

After Devon posted her ad, more than sixty messages flooded her voice mail. "Now, I don't know if that's a normal number, high or low, but there were certainly some winners, let me tell you. Some of these guys sounded bizarre, some made me laugh, some I almost cried when I heard what they had to say, and some were just plain wacko, but I answered one," she says. "This guy was a total goofball. He started singing, 'Why do birds suddenly appear,' and it was so sweetly dorky that I had to return his call, just to see who this guy was. He was a nice guy, and we dated a bit before it ran its course."

When that fizzled, Devon tried to meet people by placing personal ads online, a technique through which she met several dates. "I was dating a *lot*. I think I was giving my parents a daily heart attack. My dad actually came and found me on one blind date when I didn't return home at a reasonable hour and thoughts of different kinds of horrible deaths became too much for him to bear. Yeah, I can look back and laugh *now*," she says. "Eventually I had spent so much time dating, blindly looking for my knight in shining armor, not wanting to narrow it down because you never know when something better may come along, that it got tiring. It was tough trying to keep names and dates straight and still managing to keep my sanity and my job. The dating thing seriously became a full-time job."

Weary of meeting dozens of guys whom she couldn't see herself with long term, Devon decided to focus less on her love life and more on other aspects of her life, like her job. Soon afterward, a group of her college classmates and older alumni who had performed together in the school's drama department got together for a mini-reunion. "I had just decided to tone it down when I went to the reunion and reconnected with a guy I'd had a crush on since freshman year in college. I knew it was going to be something different this time," Devon says. "Two years later we're still together. I've never had anything like this before. It took me awhile to get to this one wonderful relationship, which I stumbled into completely by accident. I'm now 27, and I'm in such a different place than when I was 22 and starting my dating marathon. I think it's easy to look around and freak out that everyone around you is pairing off, but if it's not meant to be, it just isn't. You really have to go inward and think, 'Am I happy?' and find things that make you happy (besides a lover). It was then that I found my boyfriend, not before, when I was looking so hard. Fate has a funny way of working her magic."

More Ways to Conquer

This is not one of those questions for which there's a magic answer, as much as we all wish there was. So I have just a few items to add to the suggestions the mentors for this question offered.

Be Flexible

Many twentysomethings have told me that having "checklists" can be dangerous. It's one thing to be choosy about whom you date, and that's fine. But it's another to narrow down the qualities of the person whom you *think* you want to a list so specific that the person might not even exist. By limiting your search to people who fit into highly specific categories, instead of increasing your chances of finding someone compatible, you're only closing off opportunities. On some traits, of course, you shouldn't compromise: if you don't want someone who smokes, that's understandable. But to rule out other broad categories, like divorcees or "nonprofessionals," without knowing the individual circumstances, could be a mistake. You just never know the qualities that will click until you get to know a person. I know many twentysomethings who discovered that the person whom they ultimately ended up with fit few to none of the checklist qualities they thought they wanted.

Use Your Resources

Besides keeping an open-minded attitude, the twentysomethings I've interviewed also have a variety of creative suggestions for how to meet people. The most common way twentysomethings meet potential boyfriends or girlfriends is through friends of friends, whether they are set up or happen to meet at a party or other social gathering. One popular way to create these opportunities is to host or attend a party to which each friend invited must also bring another single person of the opposite sex. One positive aspect about our generation is that dating has become so casual that whether we are trying to meet someone or are lucky enough to have met someone, we don't always have to worry about planning an elaborate evening. Sometimes just hanging out can suffice, and eventually we'll happen to hang out with the right person.

Chapter 7

How important are sparks?

Whenever you see that person, your boyfriend or girl-friend, your one and only, your knees buckle. Buzzing sparks course through the very fiber of your being. Overdramatic music hums through your head like the climax of a bad Kevin Costner movie. The butterflies—ah, the butterflies!—lift you like an over-used metaphor. You float. You beam. You gush. You know.

Or not.

And now back to reality. The truth for many twentysome-things is that whether your relationship is good or great, some-times you get that sinking feeling in your stomach telling you that you're just not sure if you've found The One. You wonder if there's someone better out there or if you're settling by staying in your present relationship. If this were it, would you be questioning yourself in the first place? But then again, if you were to break up, would you be chasing something unattainable? Are your standards too high? Is it compromising to stay with someone who isn't a per-fect match? Does one exist? Do sparks? The next two chapters ad-dress these ideas: first, the role sparks should play; and second, in chapter 8, how you know if you've found The One.

Bailey Hamilton, 23, has been asking herself this question

nonstop in recent months. Will was one of her closest friends since they met during their first week in college. Three years later, when Bailey ended a relationship, she and Will started dating. "I decided that after the bad boyfriend (to whom I was nevertheless very attracted), I should just focus on being with a good person, because that was what would matter in the long run," Bailey says. "Will, one of my best friends, wanted the relationship. I decided to give it a try, even though he'd never given me butterflies in the stomach. He is a truly brilliant, amazing person who makes me laugh and who would never do anything to hurt me. He's getting his doctorate in bio-physics, for God's sake. He's not bad on the eyes, either. All around, he's exactly the kind of person little girls are raised to want to end up with: kind, good looking, smart, and going to be successful."

Bailey and Will have just moved in together, but Bailey can't help agonizing over whether those butterflies are crucial. "This has been a big issue for me lately. We have a gorgeous apartment. Everything looks great. I'm sure everyone on the outside thinks we're perfect together. And you know what? I'm really sad. I feel like we're living a lie. More specifically, I feel like I'm lying to him all the time. After all this time, I still don't feel, never really felt, those sparks for him," she says. "Things are comfortable, easy, no drama, so I let things continue. I tell myself, 'This is what an adult relationship is like. It's not like high school, where it's all butterflies and passion.' You can't expect that after a certain point. Nothing's 'new' anymore, so you don't have that nervousness or excitement. You need to grow up. This is what lasts. This is how it's supposed to be: comfortable, reliable."

Because Daniel Gray, a 27-year-old in Wichita Falls, Texas, believes sparks are essential, he hasn't dated anyone seriously in several years. "The reason is pretty weird. There are two types of women so far in my life: those who want to be with me, and women I want to be with," Daniel says. "For some reason, I'm caught hopelessly in the middle. There are no sparks with any of the women who want to be with me. That means I have a lot of friends who are girls. But it's sad because they're all amazing, quality girls. Then there are the women I pursue who are attracted to the idea of a relationship but won't let themselves go for it. I've become a proactive spokesman for 'just give it a chance,' the same way a car dealer tries to entice you into buying something top of the line. So far every single one of this type of women has ended things before anything ever got a chance to begin. It makes me want to throw up my hands and throw the whole thing away completely. I guess I'm not a very good salesman."

Sparks Can Build Over Time

MENTOR: Sahar Mokari

AGE: 24

I WISH I'D KNOWN AT 23 THAT "sparks are more than just a physical attraction; they are a deeper connection that needs time to develop."

After graduating from the University of California, Irvine, Sahar Mokari spent more than two years going on dates with men whom she met through an Iranian dating Web site. "I relied on the butterfly feeling on the first date to tell me whether or not I had an attraction for the person, but I had no success because I didn't meet anyone with real substance," Sahar says.

One day, Sahar saw a photo and profile on the Web site that sounded appealing. After exchanging e-mails for a week, Sahar and Babak met for coffee. She didn't feel sparks. "I didn't feel the initial chemistry I usually feel for someone I'm really into, but that should have told me something because everyone else I had dated was a loser!" Sahar says. "He was so sweet, and we had such great conversation that I wanted to see if sparks would fly on a later date. That next week we went out two more times, and by the end of the week, we were inseparable. Three months later we declared our love for each other. He just bought us a house, and we are planning our future together."

Sahar is thankful that she forced herself to look beyond the lack of sparks and, as a result, plans to marry the man she calls her soul mate. She says there is a different kind of spark that can develop that is much more important than the initial knee-buckling feeling on which she previously gauged her level of attraction to someone. "In this relationship, I learned to give it a chance, and I was very surprised to find out that the love of my life was there. I am so grateful for finally finding him and for being smart enough to look beyond what I usually looked for or felt. I guess the moral is if something isn't working for you (like dating men who are nice to look at but who treat you like crap), don't be afraid to try something else. Because I was willing to look beyond what I thought I was attracted to, I realized the type of man I really wanted was a sweet, caring, and giving man who I also have great physical, emotional, and intellectual sparks with."

Sparks Don't Have to Be Constant

MENTOR: Emma Wilson
AGE: 26
I WISH I'D KNOWN AT 20 THAT "there don't have to be sparks when you're washing dishes and he's on the couch, but that won't mean there won't be sparks the next day."

Emma Wilson, who has been married for three years, says that sparks are important, but that sparks in the traditional sense shouldn't be a central criterion of a relationship. "Sparks don't have to 'spark' every minute of every day," Emma says. "And other things are important, too, like carrying on a conversation in a car for two hours and not even realizing the time has passed. Like wanting to be with someone every minute you're not with them (even if they drive you crazy when you are). Or facing the fact that the person you're mad at and the person you want to comfort you are the same person. Or realizing that the person you're with genuinely wants to make all of your dreams come true, even the ones you didn't know you had, and you lie in bed at night and know that you love him all the way down to your toes."

Sometimes Sparks Can Be Crucial

MENTOR: Dina Adeli

AGE: 27

I WISH I'D KNOWN AT 26 THAT "passion is important, because when things are going downhill, if there's still passion, it can rejuvenate the relationship."

Dina Adeli found the sparks question so overwhelming that she became physically sick and broke off an engagement because of it. When she met her fiancé, she thought he was good looking but not her type. Nonetheless, when her family discovered that he was interested in her, they pushed her to go out with him. "So I did. I really enjoyed our first date even though he didn't make me nervous, I had no problem finishing my steak, and I never felt like we were the only two people in the room. In short, there were no sparks. But because he was a nice guy, came from a good family, and was highly educated, I continued to go out with him. And on our second date when we first kissed, again, there were no sparks, but it wasn't bad, either. We had a great time together, and thus this relationship continued," Dina says. "Through it all there was no passion, but I thought that was okay because he was such a great guy. Also, I continuously heard from people that those sparks everyone talks about go away anyway. What's important was that he was a good person with a good heart. I chose to believe it at the time. I had convinced myself."

Throughout the relationship, Dina constantly battled with her family and with herself as she weighed the importance of sparks. "I never felt them. No nausea, no lack of appetite, no 'I want to be with him every minute of every day,'" says Dina. "I had just gone through a year of blind dates and setups, one after another, and felt no connection to any of those men. My family was telling me I was too picky. Once my father even said something like, 'Who are you waiting for? Who do you think you are?' They felt I was throwing away these great opportunities. I heard over and over again from everyone that I was too picky. And even though I refused to settle for anything less than what I wanted, these words sunk into my head, and I began to believe them without even realizing it."

Eight months after their first date, they became engaged, and immediately the relationship changed. "Suddenly, this was it. We weren't dating anymore. This was a lifelong decision. And at that point, I couldn't lie to my heart any longer. I couldn't lie to my body. Every day, there was a constant battle between my mind and my heart. My heart wasn't in it; my heart didn't feel it. But my mind kept saying, 'But he's such a great guy,' and my mind was winning the battle until my body couldn't take it anymore. Maybe I could fool my heart for a little while, but I couldn't fool my body. I started losing weight and having anxiety attacks. And I didn't know whether this was happening because I wasn't happy or because I was nervous about getting married in general. I chose to believe the latter. And the battle continued," Dina says.

Over the next few months, as Dina and her fiancé fought frequently, her doubts grew, and she put off planning the wedding. "Every time I felt a little bit more sure of my decision to marry him, every time I was ready to take that one step forward in even looking at a bridal magazine, something would happen, we would get into a fight, and I would take three steps back, until finally, four months after we got engaged, one fight was the icing on the cake, and we broke up," she says. "The night we broke up, I cried for a long time, not because I wanted to be with him but because it was simply a sad situation, to think that you're going to spend the rest of your life with someone and then putting an end to it. But the next day, I was fine. I felt that a huge weight had been lifted from my back. I could breathe again. It's been two weeks now since we broke up and I haven't looked back. The more days that go by, the more I realize how lucky I am to be out of that relationship. I feel reborn, if that makes any sense, and I feel great. Sure, I know that once this high will go away, I'll be feeling lonely. But that's okay; I can live with lonely. What I can't live with is a life without excitement and passion for my partner. Because when times are bad, and you don't have that passion to count on, there really isn't much motivation to stay in the relationship."

More Ways to Conquer

The questions in this chapter and the one that follows are entirely subjective questions that have no wrong answers. Now stop and read that again because you probably read the cliché without thinking about it. *There are no wrong answers*. What that means is that sparks for one person can mean something completely different than sparks for another person. For some twentysomethings, sparks entail the knee-buckling swoons that pop out of a movie screen. For others, sparks merely translate to warm, fuzzy feelings. If you believe in and are happy with the latter, for example, there's no need to feel like you're missing out on something if you don't experience the former. If you believe in the knee buckles, that doesn't mean you have to experience them all the time. *There are no wrong answers*. Dina said that with her first boyfriend, she never felt sparks: "No nausea, no lack of appetite, no 'I want to be with him every minute of every day.'" But others of us might believe in only part of that definition: if we *do* want to be with that person every minute of every day, it might not matter if we don't, say, get nauseous or lose our appetite.

To have chemistry with someone can mean to be insanely attracted to that person, or highly compatible, or best friends with oomph. It can be something you notice on a first meeting or something that develops as you get to know each other. If you love someone but the chemistry is missing, you may have to take the difficult step of breaking up. But if the only thing that's missing is a constant Hollywood knee buckle and the only reason you miss it is because the movies tell you to, you may want to examine your own personal definition of sparks and the role you want them to play in your relationship.

Chapter 8

How do I know if I'm dating The One?

Once we're in a serious relationship, we begin to ask the broader and more pervasive question of whether we've resolved the sparks issue. It's one of those Big Questions that seems to have gargantuan ramifications for the rest of our lives. Celeste Phillipe, a 26-year-old from Pasadena, loves her boyfriend, whom she has been dating for almost a year. They have great sex, their conversations are stimulating, and they like each other's friends. "We talk about deep things, and all thoughts shared are acceptable because we count each other as safe and trustworthy. He loves me to pieces, and I know it. We have a loving, caring, supportive relationship, but I feel like something's just not right. He seems certain I am The One, and I'm not so sure. What if he's right and I'm just messed up?" she says.

Throughout college, Xavier Williams, a 1999 graduate of the University of Delaware, hooked up with a number of different girls without having a serious girlfriend. "I didn't really become emotionally attached to any of those whose names I actually knew, but I always had a feeling deep down inside that maybe I really did want a girlfriend. I just never met a girl who I felt was worth sacrificing the things that I enjoyed the most, which were hanging out with my friends and basically doing whatever I wanted," Xavier says. "This sort of behavior continued during my first year after college, only now I had a career instead of classes, and I was meeting a bunch of new girls and friends. One night I finally met a girl at a bar who I felt was good enough to pursue as a potential girlfriend, and I began to date her and got really close to her over the next six months. Now, I had never dated a girl longer than six months prior to this, and I found out that there are a lot of good and bad things involved in long-term relationships. This girl eventually became my girlfriend, and we went on to date for about three years and even lived together for a while. But at some point during that time, I began to think that even though I cared deeply for this person, she wasn't The One I wanted to spend every waking moment with for the rest of my life."

Xavier broke up with his girlfriend and moved out of the place they shared. For a time, he dated and/or hooked up with a string of new girls who were fun and attractive. And then he met a girl he truly cared about and began to date her seriously. "The dilemma I now face is how do I know if I'm doing the right thing or if I should just continue to try to hook up with as many girls as I can while I'm young and then worry about looking for my soul mate or whatever when I get older? I guess it all comes down to how do I really know if I am doing the right thing by sacrificing my youth to date someone who may or [may] not be The One?"

Use the "Smile Test"

MENTOR: Eileen McCarthy
AGE: 30
I WISH I'D KNOWN AT 26 THAT "you *can* rely on your instincts."

Eileen McCarthy asked herself this chapter's question several times over the course of a four-year relationship with a boyfriend before she was able to come up with a way to gauge whether he was The One. "I kept thinking that he loved me and it would all work out," she says, "until I was maid of honor in a friend's wedding and saw the way her groom smiled at her. Knowing my boyfriend would never smile at me that way made me cry. I couldn't imagine him smiling at our wedding. Later, when it ended, I decided I would wait for that smile. I'd love to say at the end I found the guy who had that smile. I'm still looking, but God knows I'm not going to get married without it."

Now Eileen uses the "smile test" whenever she finds herself wondering whether she is dating the man she should spend her life with. "I'm single and 30, but I have a ton of friends who've found their partners, and I guess I can say I believe it's all in the smile. The relationships that work out have a smile that seems to come from within. You can tell a lot about how he smiles at you, how you smile at him. Look at the pictures; you'll know the couples where there's trouble. We all know it. So trust the smile and trust yourself," Eileen says.

Keep an Open Mind

MENTOR: Pari Kumar

AGE: 27

I WISH I'D KNOWN AT 22 THAT "I would end up with the perfect person for me. I wouldn't have worried so much!"

As soon as Pari Kumar graduated from Rutgers University in 1998 and didn't immediately head to graduate school, she instantly felt the pressure to get married. She says, "I'm a second-generation Indian woman, and while our parents don't expect the strict arranged marriage as much anymore, there's still the strong expectation that our life partners will be Indian (preferably from the same region and language), educated, and generally, from the same class level. I saw college friends and acquaintances drop like flies, marrying the 'right way' and starting comfortable, 'approved of' lives. What scared me was that life and that way of marrying made my stomach turn. It wasn't for me."

The idea of The One fascinates Pari, who says it only adds to the stress of finding someone. "There's so much pressure behind those two words that it seems to force bad relationships; either you try really hard to make who you're dating an ideal person, or you give up on finding The One and date someone else while feeling guilty on some level about settling. When I was in my teens, my idea of The One was a hot guy, about 6'2", who was smart, could cook, and could sing opera. And of course, Indian."

But Pari's idea of The One has changed as she's changed over the past few years. "The most significant way it has changed is that I don't use that label anymore. How can a fixed, static One exist when everyone is constantly changing, especially in their 20s? I've always thought that your 20s were like dog years, that each year after college, of true independence, is equal to seven years of experience," she says. If you're still in your drama-queen stage, would you even know what to do with The One?"

Now engaged to a man whom Pari calls "an amazing fit for me," she has discovered that her notions of The One, and her parents' notions of The One for her, were all wrong. "Turns out what I needed was *not* an idealistic image of an opera-singing, culinary-talented man who fit my parents' idea of the right ethnicity for me. What I needed was a secure, intelligent, well-rounded man who can read my mind at times, takes amazing care of me, and still understands and respects that I'm an independent, outspoken, ambitious woman. Oh yeah, and the 6'2", hot guy part came true. Some things don't change. The catch? He's American," she says. "We're in the middle of wedding planning right now, and despite the stress, the looks we sometimes get from both communities, and future worries like raising well-balanced children, he's worth it. Our relationship is worth it."

Be Prepared to Date "The Many"

MENTOR: Andro Hsu
AGE: 27
I WISH I'D KNOWN AT 23 THAT "you should look for happiness in life itself, not just in another person."

When Andro Hsu was in his early 20s, he dated several women whom he pretty much knew didn't have long-term future potential. "I guess there was this sense of unease or guilt sometimes, like I didn't feel comfortable or fully myself around them. It was fun and all, but I think I was suppressing thinking about what things would be like in the future. Or maybe somehow my heart knew they weren't The One, but I wasn't listening. But usually I would try to stay together more for the sake of having a relationship—that is, a physical one—rather than doing what was best for me as a person," he says.

Because Andro explored so many relationships, when The One did show up in his life, he not only was ready for her but also recognized her as The One fairly quickly. "For me, I was only able to know I was dating The One by dating The Many. I thought I was in love with many of those women, but only in hindsight do I realize that it was merely infatuation, not love. So what's infatuation? I think when you're infatuated, you see only the good things about someone but are blind to the negative things or the characteristics that would make a real relationship unfeasible. On the other hand, The One is someone whose positive and negative traits you know intimately well because you have taken the time to know them, and you love The One precisely *because* of all the positive and negative things together, not despite them," Andro says. "With The One I'm dating, the love between us is not only for who we are, but for who we can grow to become, our potential together. When I think of my girlfriend and me, there is more than just the sum of our individual parts; there is the potential for growth on both our parts, growth which might not take place if we weren't together. And I love that potential us as much as I love my girlfriend for who she is now. I'm sure there are others out there who don't have to date The Many in order to find their One, but this is how I know I have found the One for me."

Andro's advice for twentysomethings pondering whether they're dating The One is to figure out whether that person can help you grow and improve as a person. "It's great to be with someone who likes you for your strengths, but it's much more special when that someone also knows your weaknesses, accepts them, and wants to help you improve upon them. And of course, it's even better, and only tolerable, if they can do this in a way that's not patronizing, controlling, or demeaning. Lastly, you should be able to do this for him or her as well. That's a lot to ask, but for me, the only way to get over my fears of long-term relationships is to imagine that the relationship will be even better in the future than it is now," he says.

More Ways to Conquer

If you're asking yourself whether you'll ever find The One, it could be for a number of reasons. You could simply be beginning to think about a long-term future with the person you're dating. Or you might be doubting the relationship, thinking that if this person is *not* The One, then you're wasting your time. It's that sense of uncertainty that can cause us to doubt ourselves into a frenzy—the hallmark of the Quarterlife Crisis—as we try to discern whether we're only staying together with someone because we're afraid to break up.

What if you know you love the one you're with, but only want to get a better sense of whether this is the lifelong person for you? I've heard several general suggestions for how to weigh the possible future of your relationship, among them picturing yourselves together as 80-year-olds at the dinner table and gauging how happy you are, assessing whether this is a face you can wake up to every morning, and imagining if you had a child who acted exactly like the person you're dating.

If list writing is something you find helpful to solve problems, you can try making lists to figure out whether you're with someone because you should be or because you're scared to be alone. Try writing down the reasons you should and shouldn't be with this person, things you love and don't love about him or her, and the pros and cons of staying together. Then tear the lists up, burn them, or eat them. You don't need them anymore. The act of expressing these doubts, rather than letting them fester in your mind, should relieve some of the pressure and allow you to relax. Then you're free to merely let things happen and respond to them accordingly.

Chapter 9

How do I know if I was just experimenting
or if I'm really gay or bi?

On several occasions during college, Ellen Harrington,
a 23-year-old in Little Rock, Arkansas, hooked up with other
women. At the time, the experiences didn't lead her to any broad
self-analysis. She was just having fun. But now that she is out of
college and questioning everything else about her life, she wonders
how to tell if her hookups indicate something serious about her
sexuality other than she previously realized. "I liked the girls I was
with in college, and I still find some girls attractive now, even
though I've only had a serious long-term relationship with a guy,"
she says. "I'd be open to having a relationship with a girl if that's
being true to who I am, but how do I know if I was being true to
myself in college or if I was just fooling around?"

Place Yourself in That Environment

MENTOR: Cecelia Rosen
AGE: 27
I WISH I'D KNOWN AT 21 THAT "you don't have to have your mind
made up."

When Cecelia Rosen was in college, she dated or hooked up with several men and women. On her campus, the bisexual scene was comfortable and accepted. "It seemed to be a natural thing, like hooking up with boys. I didn't think I was gay because I liked boys, too. It was just something I was open to, and the idea that this was taboo excited me. In a room full of people I could just as easily be checking out a girl as I could a guy. And the lines of boys and girls were definitely blurred for me. I was going through so much stuff on a personal level because I wasn't like my conservative friends outside of college. I was a lot artsier, a freethinker. The whole thing was a package deal; I wasn't questioning only my sexuality. I was questioning my whole individuality."

After college, Cecelia questioned her lifestyle because at the company where she worked, she noticed a lesbian coworker felt she had to be guarded about her sexuality. "Early on when I started working there, she noticed the alternative vibes I put out, and she started playing those games like, 'Oh, do you like Ani DiFranco? Indigo Girls?' But she always spoke so carefully non-gender-specific about her partner that it was weird. I saw how guarded she had to be and that it took a lot of work. At that point I was dating a girl, but I knew it wasn't serious. Then when I started Internet dating, I put on my profile that I was bi. I started getting a lot of really dirty e-mails like 'My wife and I . . . , or 'What other kinky shit are you into?' I realized people had all these preconceived notions about bis, when I was just looking for someone to connect with, and I became aware that it would be an easier path if I lived a more heterosexual lifestyle," Cecelia says. "But that wasn't me. If I found someone I connected with, it didn't matter if it was a boy or girl. When people ask what I am, I like to say it doesn't matter. I'm human (but if I *had* to label myself, I am bi). Now that I've been dating a guy for more than a year, people ask me things like, 'How do you know you won't meet a girl you're interested in and leave your boyfriend?' The question's silly. There are no guarantees in life. How do I know I won't find another guy I'm interested in? For me, it becomes more about the personality than the gender. I'm still attracted to both sexes, but the person I've connected with, someone who I'd like to have in my life for a long time, happens to be male."

Cecelia advises twentysomethings who are asking this question to place themselves in various situations and environments in which their sexuality would come into play. "Go to places like gay organizations or coffeehouses that cater to homosexual crowds. Hang out in the environment. Do you like the environment? Are you comfortable there? When people of the same sex come on to you, does that make you happy? Anxious? Do you look at it as a one-time thing? You could be straight but have one person of the same sex whom you happened to be attracted to, but for the most part you're attracted to the opposite sex. It's easy to flip it and put yourself in a straight environment. You just step out into the world, and ta-da, there you are."

Acknowledge the Signs

MENTOR: Graham Boettcher
AGE: 30

I WISH I'D KNOWN AT 20 THAT "coming out would be as easy and painless as it has been."

Graham Boettcher, a 30-year-old grad student at Yale University, came out of the closet as an openly gay man only two years ago. "In high school, when other guys were content to look at *Playboy* and *Penthouse,* I sought out more explicit pornographic magazines, like *Hustler,* for the simple reason that they featured nude men (albeit in 'straight' encounters with women). I didn't muster the courage to buy a gay porn magazine until the summer before my senior year at Yale. I had spent the summer working in Germany and had the chance to travel around Europe. While waiting for my train in Cannes, I had a good amount of time to kill and was intrigued by a porn shop across from the train station. My heart was beating so quickly when I walked through the door of the store and approached the man at the counter to purchase tokens for the video booths. The video booths played about twenty channels of porn, both straight and gay, continuously. At first, I surfed past the gay porn; it seemed *so* taboo. But eventually, I succumbed to my curiosity, and my first time witnessing man-on-man sex was a revelation. Now, I not only suspected I was gay—I *knew* it. Throughout the rest of that summer, on weekend visits to Berlin, I sought out gay porn in the so-called *Wünsch kabine* (literally 'wish cabins,' video booths) of the city's sex shops."

Until he came out, these videos were the only way Graham allowed himself to express his sexuality. "I didn't go to gay bars or put myself in any social situation where I might be outed as gay. In fact, I built my own private closet—of flesh. I allowed my weight to balloon to an extraordinary 435 pounds, knowing on some level that as long as I remained morbidly obese, sexuality would never be an issue: no man, or woman, would ever want to be with anyone so fat and unhealthy. On my 29th birthday, I took stock of my life. I was not happy. I was not healthy. I had scores of friends, but was alone. I vowed I wouldn't go another year like this, that I wouldn't turn 30 sick, tired, lonely, and closeted. The next day, I called my mother and came out to her, and in the course of the next nine months came out to my entire family (save one grandfather) and all my friends. The weight lifted from my shoulders by coming out enabled me to deal with the literal weight taxing my body. The same day I came out, I made appointments with a nutritionist, psychiatrist, and my primary care provider."

In the two years since, Graham has lost 235 pounds and two feet from his waist. Now comfortable with his sexuality, he is grateful that he finally allowed himself to interpret the signs. "I'm happier and healthier now than I have ever been. Sure, I experience the frustrations of dating and occasional heartache, but these feelings confirm that I'm alive! So how do you know if you're gay? Trust your instincts. If you find yourself exploring your sexuality abroad in ways you wouldn't at home, that probably means something. If all your erotic thoughts and dreams involve a member (or members) of the same sex, this means something, too. I ignored and suppressed my inner voice far too long, and it nearly cost me my health, physically, mentally, and spiritually."

More Ways to Conquer

Cecelia brought up an important point. The 20s are a time when we tend to question everything about our lives. So questioning your sexuality could just be part of that package. There's nothing wrong with questioning, and there's nothing wrong with feeling like you don't yet have all the information you need to come up with the answers. Many gay and bi twentysomethings, like Graham, say that deep down they knew their sexuality all along. But for others, discovering who they are sexually is a process that continues into adulthood. For still others, a sexual label is of no importance; they are happy to find romance with a personality, regardless of gender.

One gay twentysomething I met had a simple test that he recommended. In as PG-13 a way as I can put it here, he said, "When you masturbate, do you think about guys, girls, or both?"

Or you can ask Liz Cleary, a mentor earlier in this book, who says, "Here's a great test I have discovered. If you have the following characteristics, you are truly 100 percent gay: If you are male, in your 20s, gorgeous, artistic, smart, fun, share my interests, and live in any city I could see myself living, then you're probably gay."

Part 3

Work Life

The fact that we may spend as much as 60 to 70 percent of our lives working isn't the only reason that work-related issues are probably the most common cause of a Quarterlife Crisis. Soon after graduation, it becomes clear that work will form a major part of our identity, or at least how others perceive us. After we leave the school environment, we are no longer identified by which school we attended or what we majored in. Or if we ended our education after high school, we're no longer associated with our hometown or the role we played in school (which could also be a good thing). Suddenly, it seems like we're judged quickly and succinctly by our answer to a single question, that dreaded inquiry that can leave us feeling like dirt: So, what do you do?

It sounds harmless enough, whether you hear it at a party, bar, or Great Aunt Erma's third wedding. But the question is loaded. Because the popular icebreaker implies that work equals identity, we're led to believe that what we do for a living is who we are. After all, when was the last time you responded, "I like to paint watercolors, take kickboxing twice a week, and read celebrity magazines on Mondays over lattes with my friends"? We dread the question, What do you do? because odds are we're not yet *doing* exactly what we want to do. In some cases, we have no idea what we want to be, so our current job is a fallback plan as we try to pursue another dream, or it's a much lower step on the ladder than where we want to be. And if other people, and eventually we ourselves, come to associate our identities with a job or career path that means nothing to us, our self-esteem can be crushed.

There are many who say that a job is just a job, that "work" and "fun" are two different words for an obvious reason. Twentysomethings who are able to compartmentalize that way are lucky. And it's true; a job does not make a life. But our generation has taken a lot of heat in recent years because many of us focus so intently on our desire to make a living doing something meaningful about which we feel passionate. Is it really so damningly self-indulgent to want to love what you do? Life is short. Many of us wonder what life is worth if we feel dead inside eight to ten hours a day.

It seems there are two ways to look at the work you do. Either you view your job as simply a way to make money—a way to fulfill the reality that you must earn a living to support yourself—or else you turn your work into something that somehow enhances your life. If you want more from your job than a paycheck and your current position isn't providing that, then it's time for a change. The wealth of advice and tips in the mentors' answers to the following questions will help you determine the kind of change you need and how to get it.

Chapter 10

How do I weigh doing something I love
versus making enough money?

Just because a twentysomething has found his or her
passion, the question discussed in chapter 2, doesn't mean it's easy
to figure out what to do about it. What if you know what your passion is but don't think you can make a good enough living from it?
Rachel Schneider, 29, has struggled with this question for several
years. After graduating from Purdue in 1996, Rachel went to graduate school for master's degrees in social work and Jewish studies
because she knew she wanted to work in the Jewish community. "Is
success defined by a job you're good at or how much you make to
have a life outside of work? I think about this question all the time.
I chose a program I thought would help me in the workforce because of its name and status and worked my tail off for two years,"
Rachel says. "I thought if you went to graduate school, you'd be rewarded financially. I haven't found that to be true in my field."

In her third nonprofit job in the field in five years, Rachel's
happiness with her work is tainted by the paltry salary. "I hate
that I have to think about every penny I spend. For most of my
friends, a $70 dinner is no big deal. For me, it means more debt. I
can't afford the clothes I need. I can't afford the wedding and baby
presents I'm expected to buy. I can't afford to take vacations, even

though I could take the days. It drives me crazy that I have to say no to opportunities my friends can take advantage of, like social functions and benefits. I choose to have some credit card debt, which I try to pay down," she says. "For me, the money *does* make a difference because you need money to 'live' your life. A friend told me I should get married, and it won't be a problem. But I don't want to depend on someone else for my livelihood."

Because she is earning the same salary she did when she entered her field, Rachel believes she has reached a crossroads: she must decide whether to continue in her chosen line of work and accept that she probably won't ever make a satisfying salary, or to give up and take a higher paying job. "I love what I do, but I think I'm unable to continue to do it. It upsets me a great deal. I might have to stop working in this job, and possibly the Jewish community and non-profit world, and work somewhere where I can earn money," she says. "I've had great experiences, made wonderful friends and contacts, and learned a tremendous amount. I'm wondering if sometimes you have to give up something you love doing in favor of money, and that's disappointing, but a reality, and, for me, a hard lesson to have come to terms with."

Your Job Is Not Your Entire Life

MENTOR: Andrea Davis
AGE: 27

I WISH I'D KNOWN AT 22 THAT "I have another fifty to sixty years of working life, which is a long time to figure things out."

"People who went to college with me but haven't seen me since always think I went into writing. It was definitely my love. It was the thing that made my blood rush, that made me walk faster to get home: a new story idea, an answer to a character dilemma," says Andrea Davis. "But if there was a choice to be made between what I love and money, I chose money. For now."

Andrea, who won prizes in college for her fiction-writing talent, does no creative writing in her position as a high-level banker in

Manhattan. "For me, banking was the right choice. It gave my mind the stimulation it needed and comforted my financially nervous heart; I was terrified of not having enough money. For the first six months of my job, when it was really intense, I regretted my decision and thought maybe it wasn't my calling. But I just couldn't be sure what was right for me then, and I stuck with my job out of a sense of pride. When I ranked the things I was concerned about, the number one thing for me happened to be financial security. When I thought about what made me most and least comfortable, I realized I was most comfortable when I didn't have to worry about paying the bills, and I was least comfortable when I didn't have a plan. A writing career would have been the fastest way to not have a plan," she says. "My sister is a writer, and the pressure on her To Create, to form something out of nothing, to forge a path of success with no guidelines, support network, or assurance of any kind, it's simply incredible. Me, I get up at about 7 a.m. every day and know what I need to get done. I have my bad days and good days, but I don't worry about my credit card bills or the vacation I want to take."

One way Andrea has been able to deal with the fact that her job doesn't involve her passion is by making sure that writing plays a role in her life outside of work. When she's not at the office, she often writes short stories. Two years ago she began a creative writing group of twentysomethings who get together regularly, encourage each other to write, and critique each other's stories. "I'm no less of a person because I decided not to try to make a living out of my creativity. In fact, if I were writing full time, I wonder if I would think of it with the same fondness," Andrea says. "I get a charge out of my day job, and writing for me is still a pleasure, a release, a joy I look forward to. I'm building experiences every day that I fully expect to eventually turn into stories."

Just because Andrea isn't focusing on writing now doesn't mean she won't give it a try when she feels she has accomplished what she needs to financially. "It's not a matter of in the next six months if I don't find the thing I love, then I'm ruined and the course of my life can't be redirected. I have a lot of time, so I don't need to think I'm making decisions now for the rest of my life. People often change directions, and it really is a matter of being in a certain area long enough to be able to figure out what you really think of it. I have in my mind that someday I'll stop working as much; perhaps I'll teach and even write. I could not have more respect for people who write, paint, dance, and create as their day job," she says. "I'm just not ready to join those ranks quite yet."

Scope It Out First

MENTOR: Tammy Colandrea
AGE: 28

I WISH I'D KNOWN AT 25 THAT "life isn't a race; it's a journey, a process. None of the decisions you make at 25 will make or break the rest of your life."

Tammy Colandrea's first job out of college was with a small sales marketing consulting firm that promised a steadily escalating salary if she remained with the company. But Tammy found the work unfulfilling. "I tried telling myself that my work would pay off with a nice salary," she says. "But no matter what I did, I found I was always looking for the meaning in my work. Who is this helping? Is this the best we can do for people? After a year and a half, I was physically sick of the hustle and the frequent trips out of town for business."

Tammy traded in her job for one that involved hands-on work teaching and caring for autistic children, a job with decent pay that she loved. This time, she was eager to go to work every morning and didn't mind working late or traveling for the job because the work met her emotional and financial needs. But when Tammy got married and had to move to a different city, she still wasn't sure what to do with her life. For two years she worked as a private home teacher, "which bought me time to think," she says. Tammy struggled with the decision over whether to pursue a career she thought she'd like when it wouldn't adequately support her and her new husband.

To help her with her decision, Tammy got to know several older individuals who worked in social services. "You know what? They were all okay. None of the decisions they had made in life had killed them. They were all healthy, content, and doing more than just getting by financially. And they all said the same thing: if you do what you love, the money will come. Somehow I was able to receive that. So I'm pursuing the thing I've grown to love. Because I am so committed to it, everywhere I look I see opportunities that will allow me to make money and perhaps in novel ways." Currently Tammy is studying for a degree in social work and taking those novel opportunities by looking into consulting, writing, speaking, and educational side jobs related to social service.

Tammy also suggests that twentysomethings wrestling with this issue should "do your research" by befriending people in the field and getting enough information to put together a complete list of positives and negatives of the career. "Perhaps a realistic look at the career will produce too many negatives to make it worth loving any longer. But if that's not the case, pursue it. Life is about being resilient and taking chances, making mistakes and learning from them," Tammy says. "I think this question goes hand in hand with the one that asks, 'When do I let go of my dream?' In short, you don't. I think your dream lets go of you, and until it does, it will plague you until you fulfill it in some kind of way. Never in a million years did I want to be a social worker. I certainly didn't believe I'd be spending money to pursue it. But now that I am, I couldn't be happier, and I couldn't be more at peace."

Happiness Is Worth Sacrifice

MENTOR: Lisa Crawford

AGE: 31

I WISH I'D KNOWN AT 25 THAT "you can't make a positive impact if you're not working on something you love."

When Kansas native Lisa Crawford was in her mid-20s, she accepted what she says many people would consider an ideal job.

As a public relations executive for a fiber optics company, she had an excellent salary, superb benefits, and job security. She traveled to national conferences, where she served as the company spokesperson. Because she had known she wanted to be a writer since she was 14, Lisa believed the position, which emphasized writing skills, had everything she wanted in a job.

But after two years of what amounted to technical writing, Lisa got bored. When she realized her job dissatisfaction outweighed the money and benefits, she "did some serious soul-searching," she says. "Against my spouse's better wishes, because he's motivated by money and hated to see me leave that paycheck, I resigned in the fall of 2000. I decided that nonprofit public relations was the road I'd rather travel, and anyone who understands the world of nonprofit knows that meant a major cutback in our pocketbook. But I've never regretted my decision. I work for a nonprofit agency that benefits youth and holds promise for their futures. My writing has improved tremendously, and I work harder than I ever have."

When Lisa drastically reduced her paycheck, she and her husband made efforts to cut back on luxuries by selling their four-wheel-drive truck, shopping at consignment stores, and cutting back on restaurants and entertainment. "We've lived with the bare necessities for the past three years, but we haven't suffered or gone without. And now that some of our college loans and vehicles are paid off, we see that happiness in our careers leads to happiness at home."

Lisa thinks twentysomethings dealing with this dilemma should be aware that money will not necessarily motivate your work performance. "For me, I was inspired to make a difference in youth. What inspiration is there in a fiber-optic cable? You must be driven by the impact you have on the product, not the money. I think it's funny that many car salespeople don't drive the model they sell. If I want the buyer to believe in my product, then I should also be a user of it. Because I enjoyed my new career, I worked diligently and was promoted to VP after eight months.

In the corporate world, the only way up the ladder is with some major sucking up."

More Ways to Conquer

It seems that a good guideline to help you answer the question, How do I weigh doing something I love versus making enough money? would be to ask yourself, "If I had to choose one or the other, what would make me happiest: financial stability, with the lifestyle that comes with it, or a job that I would love doing for eight or more hours a day?" The question is subtly different from the one that heads this chapter. If financial stability or success could in itself make you happy, or if a lack of a well-off lifestyle makes you unhappy, as it does Rachel, perhaps your answer is clear.

You Can Separate Work from Passion

In that case, Andrea's story gives us another crucial answer to this issue: you can still do what you love outside of your day job. Andrea has figured out how to have both a well-paying job *and* writing, something she loves, in her life, and doesn't feel like she is missing out on aspects of either. In fact, this situation is rarely either/or; you don't have to choose between, say, a desk job or dancing. Not only can you do both, as Andrea has, but also the time you spend at one activity may rev you up for the other, and your time-management skills might improve because you understand the importance of including both activities in your life.

You Have a Lifetime to Fit It All in

Another crucial factor to weigh is time. How desperately do you need to do what you love, eight-plus hours a day, for a living, *right now*? Tammy's stable job was making her feel sick; if a job makes you that miserable or physically affects you, it makes sense to leave. But it's also possible to find a middle ground, a tolerable job that will pay you now while you explore the options to do what you love at a later time. One of Andrea's consolations is that she doesn't expect to remain a banker for the rest of her life. She doesn't view this question as one of loving her work versus making money. She realizes that there is time to do both in her life, and she doesn't necessarily have to do them both simultaneously.

Decide What's Worth Giving up

If, however, you conclude that doing what you love is more important than financial stability, and that it *has* to be all or nothing, then you have a different set of questions to weigh. First, Do you love it so much that you're willing to sacrifice important things and indulgences? Will you sacrifice (at least for the time being) time, sleep, and energy? A social or romantic life? Material goods? If it's not worth it to you to make those sacrifices, then perhaps you don't love it as much as you thought you did, or maybe there's something else you'll love that can accommodate your lifestyle. Rachel mentioned not being able to afford vacations, dinners with her friends, and certain wedding and shower gifts. She needs to decide whether those aspects of her life are more important than doing exactly what she loves. (Her statement, "You need money to 'live' your life," might serve as a clue for her.)

Get at It from Another Road

But even if someone like Rachel leans toward the financial angle, she doesn't necessarily have to give up what she loves. Is there another position in the same field, though with slightly different responsibilities, that pays better? Perhaps there are ways to work in the field that you haven't thought of. If none exists, maybe you can create them by adding responsibilities to your job or expanding the community you serve.

Earn Creative Income

If you love what you do more than you love other aspects of your life—if you are willing to sacrifice to pursue your passion professionally, then there are always things you can do to save money while you pursue what you love full time, as Tammy found. Easy answers include saving money by taking the bus or walking, and packing your own lunch. An answer that doesn't always come to mind is that it's possible to consider earning money in various untraditional ways to supplement the base salary of the job you love. You might think about less structured ways of making cash on the side. Some publishers, for example, pay people to proofread final manuscripts. Most cities have centers for focus groups, where companies pay for your opinions. Perhaps you have a skill that you can use on a freelance basis: fixing cars, copyediting documents, or playing piano accompaniment. And don't underestimate the occasional babysitting gig; going rates for our age group are about $15 an hour.

You *can* do what you love and make enough money to survive. You just have to decide what's worth sacrificing to get there.

Chapter 11

Will I always hate going to work?

Leigh French, 28, worries that she will always hate going to work, no matter where she is. "I dread going to work. I have a fairly new job and thought that my dread was just my last job, but it's not. I just hate going to work. I don't love what I do, and I don't know what I would love to do in terms of work, which could be the problem," she says. "What I hate more than going to work is people asking if I like my job. They don't appreciate my honesty when I say no, and I don't lie very well. I wonder if I will ever find that job that I enjoy. My fiancé loves what he does. He's passionate about his work. How does that happen? I know I'd be bored at home all day, and it's not that I don't want to work; I just want a job I can go to and feel passionate about. I dread Sunday nights because they mean Monday morning is only a pillow away. I don't want to be 50 and still hate going to work."

Life Is Too Short

MENTOR: Iain Watson
AGE: 26

I WISH I'D KNOWN AT 23 THAT "it's better to be poor and happy than rich and miserable."

For four years, Iain Watson worked as a commission controller for a large international insurance company in Edinburgh, Scotland, because the job paid well and his family considered his career path to be "lifelong" and respectable. "I had a very hard time in my mid-20s because I absolutely hated the job. Every day I used to ask myself why I was doing it and gave the same answer: security and respectability," Iain says. "However, I was miserable. I found myself becoming increasingly bitter and cynical towards everyone, and I couldn't hold on to a partner for any length of time."

In September 2001, Iain planned to take off work for a month-long vacation in New York. His flight was scheduled for September 13th. "That all changed on September 11th. The next day I went in to work, handed in my notice, and walked out. I just realized life is too short," he says. "I had a month's salary, so I asked myself what did I really want to do with my life. The answer was staring me in the face. I've always been technologically minded (in my previous job I worked in an engineering firm), but I've also always loved films and actually did a two-year film studies course at school. So I decided to completely switch careers."

Iain worked out a game plan to get a job where he wouldn't hate going to work. He hoped to become a cinema projectionist, work his way up to chief projectionist, land a chief position at a cinema in the West End of London ("the busiest cinemas in the world"), and eventually become an audio technician or installation engineer. He wrote to every movie theater in Edinburgh a letter explaining the entry-level job he sought. Fortunately, a new multiplex had just opened. The administrators had filled all of the projection staff positions but told Iain he could compete for a job as a trainee projectionist. Iain beat out the twenty-one other applicants, only to find that his job entailed menial tasks for low pay. But he worked hard anyway. When after three months he heard that another theater in the city had a projectionist shortage, he applied for the job and is now a full-time projectionist.

Although Iain's salary is much lower than the paychecks he earned at the insurance company, Iain considers himself lucky to have landed where he is now. "I love what I do, I actually enjoy going in to work, and my attitude in life in general has improved dramatically. I've made a lot more friends and hold down relationships for longer than a week," Iain says. "Will you always hate going to work? If you're doing something that doesn't interest you or stimulate you, yes, you will. I stuck at my old job for four years. If I didn't have that sudden revelation, I most probably would have still been sitting at my old desk to this day, feeling miserable."

Work Is a Lifestyle

MENTOR: Katie Carter

AGE: 28

I WISH I'D KNOWN AT 22 THAT "you'd be shocked at how many successful people who seem fully confident actually have tons of insecurities about their work."

When Katie Carter, a marketer in Florida, was in a six-month funk over whether she was in the right job, she was gradually able to discern something crucial. She realized that her visceral reaction to the intensity of her job didn't necessarily have to do with the job itself. She says, "It was my first job, which was a change in environment and comfort zone. It was the first time I had to meet someone else's deadline. It was so different from college, where you set the rules and the standards. At work, someone else is telling you that you have to be there at eight in the morning, and, no, you can't go running in the middle of the day. I realized I was uncomfortable with and hated the working life, less so the actual job."

Eventually, when she became accustomed to the hours and the lifestyle, she realized she actually liked what she was doing. When she was having a bad day, she had a strategy to get through it. "Even when I was having a really tough day, I thought of it the same way as if it were a relationship: I thought of it as an adventure. I would say, 'Okay, today's a challenge, but I will have something at the end of it' and tried to pick myself up that way," she says. "Many times what liking the job came down to was confidence, a feeling of whether or not I'm really good at something. I want to tell twentysomethings this, especially the junior people who work under me who ask me things like, How did you get to be like you are, someone who speaks really well, has a strong presence in meetings, and is confident? What I want to tell them is you will always look at someone else and think they have everything going for them, but when you talk to them one on one, you might learn they have every single insecurity and confusion and lack of direction you think you have. Nobody has it as together as they seem to. So try to take comfort that you're not sitting alone in your own little boat that's rocking in the waves. We're all sitting in our own little boats, and we're all rocking. In your job, you're learning something, and if worst comes to worst and you really don't like it, you will move on to something else."

Get Over It

MENTOR: John Pozniak
AGE: 27
I WISH I'D KNOWN AT 25 "the winning Powerball numbers when I would be 26."

"Will you always hate going to work?" asks John Pozniak, a 1999 Salisbury University graduate. "Yes. It is a way of life. There is a support group for it called Everyone, and they meet at the bars on Friday. If it was all sugar and cookies, why would anyone retire? The key is to find a job that doesn't suck 'as bad.' The good thing is since your job sucks, everything else you do seems that much better and more rewarding. A candied apple isn't as sweet when it's given to you as when it's something you work for.

And after a long day's work, how good does a beer taste? Going on vacation, buying a home, these are all things you can't accomplish without a job. Plus, how nice is it to sleep in on a Saturday? Wouldn't be the same if you did it every day; it would lose its luster. Work is like a hangover. People should learn to appreciate both. I've accepted the fact that there are going to be crappy days, really crappy days, and 'eh, today wasn't so bad' days, but, honestly, that's why work is called work and not called 'fun' or 'naked Twister with the Swedish bikini team.' "

More Ways to Conquer

Aside from a noticeable lack of Swedish bikini teams, there are scores of possible reasons for a twentysomething to hate going to work, but they generally narrow down to a few possibilities. If you hate going to work, you'll need to isolate which factor or factors are at the root of the cause rather than let one negative aspect of your job taint the entire field for you. For example, I've heard from several young lawyers in large firms who feel obligated to practice law so they can pay back their exorbitant student loans, but they told me they hate going to work. By the time I heard from them, they were weighing whether to stay in a job they hated until they were able to pay back their debt or to jump to an entirely different field.

At first I was surprised that these twentysomethings didn't even mention a middle ground, but since then I've heard many stories from people our age who forget to separate their feelings toward a job from their feelings toward a field. So I recommend that twentysomethings take some time to think hard about a question to help them sort out their feelings:

What, Specifically, Do You Hate About Work?
Is it the particular company you don't like, the kind of work you're doing, the people you're working with, the city you're working in, the lifestyle of your position, or the entirety of your field?

(For the lawyers, this translated to, Is it the particular firm you don't like, the type of law you're practicing, the people you're with, the city in which you work, the hours you're working, or the act of lawyering?)

Once the lawyers thought, really thought, about separating these aspects of their work, I heard a variety of answers that illustrated the importance of separating the job from the field. One, for example, wasn't happy with his firm and the way it treated associates, but he found the other aspects of his job tolerable. Once he found a similar position at another firm, he was much happier going to work. Another didn't like the kind of law he was practicing. When he was able to convince the partners to switch him to a different practice within the firm, his job satisfaction skyrocketed. Another couldn't stand the cold days in Boston, so he transferred to an office in another city. Again, a sudden change of attitude.

Can You Make Work Better?

Another common reason twentysomethings initially balk about going to work is the culture shock of the monotonous desk-job routine: wake up early, commute (bus, subway, car), sit behind desk, sit behind desk, sit behind desk, meeting, sit behind desk, commute (bus, subway, car), sleep, repeat. Many of us merely need to get used to the routine, as did Katie, and will find that eventually the process will fade to the background of our working lives as we get more involved in and enthused about the work itself. If after years of this, the routine still sends you into the "this can't be the rest of my life" panic, you *do* have other options.

Change Your Routine

First, if you like the work itself, or at least the path that the work will eventually lead to, it's definitely worth asking your employer if you can work out a different arrangement. Companies today understand much more than they did ten years ago that our generation doesn't put a whole lot of stock in "face time." Rather than prove we're doing our job by sitting at the office for a prescribed number of hours during a required time frame (9 a.m. to 6 p.m., 8 a.m. to 8 p.m., etc.), many of us would rather have a project-based scenario: as long as we do the work by the time it's due, it doesn't matter where we do it. Ask your supervisor if you might be able to telecommute a certain number of days per week. Or suggest a comp-time or flex-time arrangement in which you can bank extra hours you work on one day and take them off on another day. If your boss is open to it, you can even come up with your own creative ideas: work late on Wednesdays in order to take Friday afternoons off, for instance. It's worth asking your employer or potential new employers about the possibility of these arrangements. One twentysomething I know disliked his job until he requested to telecommute three days a week, and his boss agreed. He still gets the work done, but three days a week he does it from home, which makes a huge difference in his lifestyle and his attitude.

Will you always hate going to work? Not if you work up the courage to make the necessary changes. The next chapter will help you figure out when the time is right to make the biggest of these moves.

Chapter 12

When do I give up on a job?

"I don't know of anyone who worries about Quarter-life Crisis stuff more than me," says a Massachusetts performer who goes by the name "Stash." "I found this question painful and terrifying because the topic really hit me. I work in a call center and I'm a redundant unit of information at work. I'm there at my cubicle, or as they call it here, 'pod.' I'm there because someone disliked the voice-automated system or they couldn't figure it out because they were too old or too adverse to technology, and they pressed # to get me."

Stash has worked in the call centers of several companies throughout the past decade. "It doesn't really matter which company you take calls for because they're all about the same. You get a cubicle, old headphones, and a PC. I am number 1236. They always know where you are and what you're doing (which is why my favorite show is the 1960s program, *The Prisoner*). You must be careful what you say to customers because you're being taped and sometimes monitored. You don't want to talk to customers too long because it'll make your average call-handle time too long, but you can't be rude and get rid of them, either. Customers are often irate and want a supervisor who doesn't want to talk to them. You can't sneak off the phones to take a leak or smoke a butt. This job has no goals, no meaning. You can't tell one day from the next. And you know it's only a matter of time before technology will render you, the human being, obsolete."

Stash wants to leave his job but doesn't know when or how to give it up when it funds the very different life he leads at night. During the day, Stash goes by his real name and miserably answers calls. At night, Stash sings blues songs and does stand-up comedy at local clubs. "At night, no one knows my real name. I guess I've developed another identity to deal with the fact I hate my job. But you can't escape reality; it penetrates everything, even my night-time persona. I'm stuck between two identities. That horrifies me. I hate to admit that. Why can't I focus on one thing or the other? I'm totally lost not knowing when to give up my day job. When will I grow up?"

Don't Compromise Yourself or Your Goals

MENTOR: Lisa Stratton
AGE: 24
I WISH I'D KNOWN AT 22 THAT "no opportunity is a good opportunity if you're treated poorly. Do what you feel is right."

When Lisa Stratton moved from her Midwestern hometown to New York City, she scored two terrific internships that left her feeling optimistic about her blossoming PR career. When the second internship ended, she accepted a job with a small PR company that seemed to offer her great opportunities to advance. But she quickly discovered that the much-vaunted advancement opportunities had been overstated, and the job was getting her nowhere fast. "At first I stuck with it because I didn't want to ruin a potential opportunity or be seen as a job-hopper. Not only was I stuck in a dead-end position, but my superiors treated me like dirt. Even though they knew their work depended on mine, they still did everything they could to strip down my self-worth and keep me within my position, giving me no opportunity to learn new job skills. It was a disappointing situation because I went into that job feeling really great about myself," Lisa says. "Being confronted with the nature of the job and how much I wanted out made me feel like a failure."

After a period of soul-searching, Lisa finally decided to quit her job, even though she had no backup plan. "I eventually had to realize that not everything in my life would go smoothly and I would have to deal with harder choices in the future; being unemployed and happy was looking better every day. After weeks of emotional abuse, I decided no job was worth feeling like crap every day for."

Once she left the job, Lisa was unemployed in a city where she knew only a few people, but she was happier than she had been since she had taken the PR job. For two months, she diligently job hunted and contacted people whom she had networked with in the past. This time, as potential employers quizzed her, she also screened them to make sure the company was one that would give her room to grow. "Finally, I managed to land a job with a PR company that treats everyone with respect," Lisa says. "I'm glad I listened to myself because not only would I have missed the opportunity for my current job, but I also would have been compromising myself on a daily basis for people who obviously had no intention of seeing me excel. From personal experience, I'd say take a hike when you feel you have to start compromising your values and goals."

Give It a Fair Shot

MENTOR: Amanda Baretto
AGE: 26
I WISH I'D KNOWN AT 25 THAT "you shouldn't give up so easily, and don't take your job so seriously."

Sometimes, however, it takes awhile at a job to figure out whether you should throw in the towel. When recent MBA graduate Amanda Baretto was hired for a sought-after job by a finance degree candidates, an investment banking associate at a Wall Street bank, she was thrilled. The recruiters assured her that her position would be one of responsibility, prestige, and excitement, accompanied by a large paycheck. "After only a few short months of working at my chosen company, I began to uncover some truths about investment banking," Amanda says. "First, responsibility means working over eighty hours a week and making sure every single piece of analysis you complete is perfect. Second, prestige is a matter of personal preference. Waiting for production to finish printing pitch books only so I can flip through them to make sure there are no printing errors at 3 a.m. isn't my idea of prestige. Third, both excitement and anxiety can cause the same physical reaction for an overworked associate. Finally, compensation has been slowly declining, and head-count reductions have been increasing."

Six months into her job, Amanda began weighing whether to leave it. She looked into other opportunities such as working as a financial analyst for one of her clients, switching divisions within the bank, or returning to the job she had before she graduated with her MBA. "But as I began to look closer at the other jobs, I realized they all seemed less interesting and challenging. I decided there was a possibility that six months wasn't a sufficient amount of time to decide whether or not this job was suited for me. Everyone knows that no matter where you start, the first few years always consist of grunt work, and the first year is a sort of initiation into the club. So I told myself I'd wait another six months, and if I still felt unhappy with my job, I'd quit. I had nothing to lose and a lot to gain. The salary was good and I was learning a lot," Amanda says. "Over the next few months, things changed. The economy improved, and more transactions came to life. I immediately began working on more interesting projects and had to do less grunt work. In fact, I enjoyed going to work in the mornings. Also, after working on some of these live transactions, I began to appreciate those recruiters' words of wisdom. After closing one transaction, I saw a *Wall Street Journal* article about this particular deal on the front page. I immediately rushed to call my parents. While dialing, I thought, 'This job really does bring responsibility, excitement, and prestige.' I'm now well past my one-year anniversary, and I can truly say I'm very happy I decided to stay. I'm not certain what the future holds, but for now, I know I made the right decision."

Amanda suggests the following four-step process for twenty-somethings struggling over whether to give up a job:

Have a game plan. "Decide how long you'd be willing to stay to see if things improve. I think that giving yourself at least six months to one year at a job is a good ballpark."

Weigh the pros and cons. "Ask yourself what you would be gaining or losing by staying an extra few months."

Examine your choices. "Look at the alternatives available to you right now, and try to compare them with what would be available six months or one year from now."

Move on. "If you still feel the same way after sufficient time has passed, it's time to move on."

More Ways to Conquer

We struggle with the question of when to give up on a job, especially when we don't have a backup in place, mainly because of a fear that we'll make a mistake. If I leave now, will I miss out on something I could have had six months from now? Will I burn bridges I might need later? What if I can't find anything better? What if I continue to get bored or frustrated six months into every new job and this becomes a pattern? I felt this way one month into a job I couldn't stand and continued to question whether to stay or go until I had been there for eight months. My major concern, I remember, was that future employers would frown on such a short stint and question the ensuing gap in my résumé. That was the only reason I stayed as long as I did.

That was back in 1998. I didn't know then that job-hopping was beginning to lose its stigma. Luckily, six years later, it's considered the norm. Thanks both to the tendency to jump for greener pastures during the dot-com boom and to the ensuing years of a dreary economic landscape fraught with layoffs, high turnover is no longer a rarity in any field. Consequently, there is no longer a standard amount of time that a twentysomething needs to stay at a job to maintain a respectable résumé, unless there's been an entire series of, say, two-month stints.

Every job—every experience—you have will teach you something about yourself, from the specific (I hate pig farming, or I can't work retail anymore) to the general (I like working outdoors, or I prefer the camaraderie of an office). Once you've learned, really learned, and there's nothing else left to learn or to like, then you can think about moving on. But unless you're in an absolutely miserable situation, you might as well give each job a fair chance, like Amanda did.

It's crucial to keep in mind the *realistic* other job possibilities that are out there for someone with the level of experience you have. When we graduate, bright eyed and ready to rumble, we might not be prepared for the realistic life of entry-level work. This is what those college career centers usually don't tell you: even if you graduate with honors and snag all the right internships, you could still spend your first few years in the working world making copies and getting other people coffee. The truth is that for most people, the 20s aren't the glamour years we expected them to be. But you need to realize that scenario is normal and common. Be sure before you leave that it's the field you dislike and not just your particular job in that field—a job that might naturally lead to something more fulfilling a few years down the road. But in general, if, like Lisa, you don't like where you see the job taking you in two years *and* if you aren't being treated humanely or respectfully (note: fetching documents and sending faxes doesn't mean you aren't being treated with respect), then leave.

If you've given your job a chance, still don't like the lifestyle, can't make changes to your working environment, and continue to hate going to work, clearly you have a new job search ahead of you. But when you embark on this search, there are a couple things to keep in mind:

Look Beyond the Obvious

There are thousands of nontraditional alternatives that might be a better fit for you than more well-known careers. When we make career choices immediately after we leave school, we haven't been exposed to most of the opportunities out there. Look through reference books in the library to get a sense of the wide variety of fields that you haven't even heard of. Ask people in specific fields about lesser known positions.

String Things Together

There is no rule that says that to earn a living we must work at one full-time job. It's possible to string together part-time jobs, (whether as a way to pursue something you love at one job while earning a steady paycheck at the other), or to prevent boredom by shifting environments, or to work from home part of the time and with the camaraderie of an office the rest of the time. Whether this is a temporary scenario or a permanent one, it's an option to keep in mind. The only reason I was able to strike out on my own as a freelance writer and speaker, for example, was because I had a steady paycheck coming regularly from my office job at a magazine.

And if that next job doesn't work out either, and the one after that, don't despair. Most twentysomethings eventually figure out a direction by trial and error, which can take a while. Job-hops—like breakups—are often necessary to teach you who you truly are and what you want in life. Any job or relationship that teaches you what you don't like is just as valuable as one that teaches you what you do. There's no reason to expect to find the right job, or even the right field, right away. You wouldn't expect to marry the first person you date, right? Look at each unsatisfactory job as a stepping-stone to something else. The stepping-stones might not directly follow each other, one above the next. Think of it more like stones in a brook, some crooked, some in the direction you want to go. Eventually you'll get somewhere new and exciting. Once you figure out where you want to go, the next chapter offers ways to move in that direction.

Chapter 13

What if I want to completely change
direction in my career?

Earlier in this book, mentors shared stories about how
they started over again. But what if you're looking to change your
career direction, specifically, and you don't know how, when, or if
you should go about doing that? When Molly McDermott was an
engineering student at Carnegie Mellon, she focused on her belief
that if she continued with the Navy ROTC program and worked
hard in school, then she would "get to have a great job, great
career, make a lot of money, and contribute as a computer engineer." Technically, she did. After graduation, she got commis-
sioned in the Navy and worked until she became "frustrated with
the 'oldness' of the Navy leadership," she says. "I felt the Navy
did not use my skills adequately and that I could do more as a
civilian."

As a systems engineer in the civilian world, Molly spent three
years excelling at work and earning a decent salary. And then "I
decided I was bored to tears with my life, I didn't like my job, and
I had a hard time going to work every day." On the side, Molly en-
rolled in a graduate school class. "We started talking about politics and international affairs, and I loved it. I really loved it. Loved
talking about it, loved writing about it, loved analyzing it. And

then I decided that this is what I wanted to do; I wanted to get into international affairs."

Now, still an engineer (and still "bored to tears") but a class away from her master's in international affairs, Molly is torn. "The big dilemma is how does a 30-year-old engineer totally change careers without sacrificing her lifestyle. And I still haven't figured this out. I have no experience, I never lived overseas (I avoided that while in the Navy), I don't speak a foreign language, I'm not yet done with my master's, and I'm not published, not known by anyone in that world," she says. "The funny part is, everything I thought I wanted when I was younger, to be an engineer, to make a lot of money, aren't things that I want anymore. And I've really begun to regret those decisions and not taking advantage of opportunities like living overseas and doing more exciting things in the Navy. I think I've found my true calling, but don't know how to get there."

You'll Get Over the Fear

MENTOR: Teale Dotson
AGE: 31
I WISH I'D KNOWN AT 21 THAT "nothing is permanent."

When Teale Dotson, a native of San Antonio, reached the peak of her career in exercise physiology, there was nothing left to shoot for. As the manager of a hospital-based fitness center, she had taken her career path as far as it would go and realized she couldn't see herself doing the same thing for the rest of her life. "What no one told me as an undergrad is that nothing is permanent. As a sophomore in college, declaring a major was the scariest thing in the world to me. Every person whom I looked up to had worked in the same field their whole career," she says. "I never knew that people changed, and things worked out for them just fine! There are a good percentage of college grads who never even go into a career in their major. Then you have folks like me who practice in that field, then decide it's time for a change."

For two years she struggled with what to do about her career. Although she was happy with her job, she didn't want to continue in that position until retirement. To go any higher in the fitness and wellness industry, Teale would have had to give up the client interaction, which was her favorite part. So she came to the conclusion that the only thing left to do was to try something completely different. "I had always been interested in health care and focused on the medically high-risk population as an exercise physiologist. Because of the current nursing shortage, I knew I'd be able to easily find a job anywhere I wanted to go in the country," says Teale, who is currently finishing up a BS program in nursing school. "It was great having all the perks of seniority in my old career, and that will all go out the window when I start over again as a nurse. I know that, and I'll have to deal with it. However, I'll work my way back up to that point. What happens if I decide I don't like nursing? Oh, well. I guess I'll try something else then."

Teale says that twentysomethings who are contemplating changing directions should simply take the plunge. "Yes, it's scary. Starting over is always scary. Wasn't it scary when you first left for college? It's the same feeling when you decide to change directions," she says. "If you're certain you want to change direction and can't afford it, take baby steps. Many people say, 'It will take me way too many years to go back and finish a different degree.' Well, in ten years you can either be complaining about the same career or starting over in the one you want to try next."

Change Is Possible

MENTOR: Geoff Puckman

AGE: 25

I WISH I'D KNOWN AT 22 THAT "it's common to not enjoy your job, and that more people want to change than those who actually do change."

After Geoff Puckman, whom we heard from earlier, graduated from college with a marketing degree in 2001, he eventually got a job working in the marketing department of a large law firm. "But it didn't feel *right*," he says. "I learned a ton at the law firm, but I wasn't pumped to go to work." For as long as he could remember, Geoff had always dreamt about opening a restaurant and bar. After two years at the law firm, he decided that it was time to go after that dream, but he had no knowledge of the industry. "I had no idea where to search, who to ask, and what to look for. I tried to figure out how I could get started but came to no conclusions. Zero. There was despair, no doubt, and it effin' hurt. I knew before I even had a job in it that I could have a successful career in the restaurant industry, but I had to get my hands dirty and had no clue how," he says.

What Geoff did next could serve as a step-by-step road map to changing direction.

Tell everyone. First, Geoff consulted family, friends, and coworkers to get leads on how to begin. He told everyone he knew that he was hoping to get into the restaurant business. It worked: a cousin happened to mention that the National Restaurant Association annual trade show was coming up in Chicago.

Learn about the field. Next, Geoff went to the trade show to get a thorough sense of the industry. "I'll be damned if that wasn't one of the best things I've done. The trade show had *everything* even remotely related to the restaurant industry: obviously food and drink vendors, but also inventory control systems, cable and music package vendors, furniture and appliance vendors, everything. It was the *perfect* way to check out the industry because I could be exposed to the entire industry," he says.

Follow every lead. Then Geoff worked his other leads. A family friend who knew of Geoff's dream told the head manager of a popular local restaurant that she knew someone who was interested in learning how a restaurant runs, with the end goal of opening his own. Impressed, the manager told Geoff's friend that while most restaurant training programs don't teach everything one would need to know to run a restaurant, he would be happy to help guide Geoff through the process.

Ease into it. For several months, Geoff worked at the law firm during the day while he eased into a job waiting tables and mixing drinks at the restaurant at night and on weekends. Then, after he had, regular hours at the restaurant, he quit the law firm. "I left a very stable and challenging job at the firm to wait tables and mix drinks. A mistake? Hell no! I'm much happier working at the restaurant because it's the path I want to head down in my quest to make Emeril look like a short-order cook at some diner," he says. "There's nothing wrong with changing direction, particularly if you're not doing something you like, and you know what it is that you would like to do. Sure, some people may think you're nuts, but hey, we're young enough to make a mistake (worst-case) and then fix it without irreversible damage."

His advice for twentysomethings is simple. "Once you figure out what you want to do, go out there and friggin' get it! No matter what it is that you want for yourself careerwise, it's not as complicated as you think, and if you're into it because it's what you want to do, you'll be willing to do what's necessary to get that job/position/what have you," Geoff says. "Sure I have friends who pull in six figures in prestigious jobs, but I don't always know if that's what they *really* want. There will be naysayers, but you'll be surprised how much respect you receive when you make a big change because it's what you want. Trust me, ladies and gentlemen, we only get to live once, so make that dream happen and enjoy it!"

It's Just a Job

MENTOR: RISA COOK
AGE: 28
I WISH I'D KNOWN AT 27 THAT "jobs are just experiences."

In 1997, the year Risa Cook graduated from Harvard, Wall Street bank recruiters were swarming the campus. Risa took a job with one of the banks. Her first few years in capital markets were fun but grew progressively less so as the markets changed. "I wasn't unhappy," she says. "I just knew that finance was never really going to be my thing, and that the longer I stayed on Wall Street, the harder it would be to extract myself from it. Finance was too intangible a world for me; it was just pushing numbers. I knew I wanted to leave finance but had no clue what I wanted to do. What happened next was sort of a fluke."

In December 2002, after six years on Wall Street, Risa happened to be helping a friend pick out an engagement ring on the showroom of her cousins' jewelry company. Risa regularly took soon-to-be-engaged friends to the store to meet with the woman who did the company's private sale business. When the woman asked Risa how she was doing, Risa replied, "Fine, but I'm ready for a change of work."

"Talk to your cousins about working here," the woman said. Risa thought about it for a month and a half. "I knew I would take a huge pay cut, but I wasn't loving what I was doing. I wasn't unhappy, but I wasn't fired up anymore. I know it's called work for a reason, but I wanted something more." Finally, Risa contacted her cousins, who hired her full time to do everything from price-tagging diamonds to developing business strategy. "People said, 'What are you doing with a degree from Harvard going to work for a diamond company?' But who really utilizes their degree? I still struggle to find people who do. I wondered if I was making a huge mistake. I had just been promoted and wondered if I could just walk away from that. And I could. I thought, *if I don't leave now, I might not ever leave, and I'll always regret not knowing if I preferred to do something else.*"

Now eight months into her new job, Risa says the most difficult part of changing directions was walking away from her Wall Street salary, but she is happy with the change. "First, it's a tangible product, diamonds; you can hold them. On Wall Street, what, are you going to be afraid that someone's going to come in and steal a hard copy of your spreadsheet? Second, everyone is fascinated by diamonds. There's a cachet because people tend to know so little about them. And the job still feels new. I have a lot to learn. The business is very technical, and very few people walk into the industry after having done something as different as I did. I walked in knowing nothing. I had a pair of diamond studs, and I didn't know anything about them."

Risa says the advice she used to make her career switch is something she'd recommend to any twentysomething contemplating a change in direction. She kept in mind something her father told her when she was a college senior trying to choose between investment banks. "My father said not only is it just a job, but it's just a first job. Hopefully it'll be a good experience, but if not, it'll still be an experience. I've kind of taken that with me. Sometimes you just have to go for it. Go with your gut. Hopefully it'll work out, and if not, try something else. To leave Wall Street, I had to make that first change. And now I know it was the right decision for me. I can visualize myself at this company ten years from now," she says. "I'm having a really good time with what I'm doing. People go to work because they have to earn a living. It's extremely rare that people are passionate about their work. It's pretty rare that they even like it. So if you like what you do, it's a bonus."

More Ways to Conquer

Often I hear that people our age feel a sometimes suffocating pressure not to change their minds. Actually, I think changing your mind is one of the most important things a twentysomething can do. Contrary to what older people might insinuate, changing your mind isn't a sign of failure or of a lack of character or direction. Changing your mind is a sign of growth. It's a sign that you are learning about yourself and getting closer to discovering who you are. Allowing yourself to backtrack opens up more avenues than forcing yourself to stick with decisions you made in the past. Essentially, being afraid to change means that you're more willing to remain unhappy than to take risks to find happiness. But if you remain in your current state, refusing to change, things aren't going to get any better. Your life isn't going to miraculously change for you unless you take steps to initiate that change.

What kind of a life will you look back on fifty years from now if you have confined yourself to one specific track and never changed direction? Because of the nature of our lives, our directions change eventually, whether we want them to or not. Unforeseen circumstances—a layoff, a baby, a natural disaster—force us to change directions at one time or another. By taking the initiative yourself, you are taking control of your change in direction, something that will help you now as well as prepare you for the times when circumstances force you to change direction. You'll be able to bounce back more quickly because you have changed directions before and know you can survive.

It does take courage to change your direction. It takes acceptance that things won't be the same. But most of all it takes resilience and strength, because you're venturing into an unknown and you might face some unexpected twists and turns. But guess what—if you are already contemplating completely changing directions, then you have already proven that you have courage, resilience, and strength. You're in a situation that isn't satisfactory, and instead of resigning yourself to a life of could've-beens, you want to change your situation. That's admirable. Now do it.

Chapter 14

Should I go back to school? or, What if school was a waste?

With the horrific economy she confronted after college graduation, Gina Maret, 24, didn't find it a difficult decision to spend a few extra semesters getting a master's degree in speech communication. She enjoyed her studies so much that now she is contemplating pursuing a PhD when she graduates. "I've become this whole new person. I think differently. I actually *think* now," she says. "Unfortunately, I never realized my working friends would begin to get married, have children, and buy homes. Suddenly, I find myself eyeing their lives jealously. My heart aches with every wedding I attend and every new baby I get to cuddle. Getting my third degree will mean postponing marriage because my long-time partner doesn't want to work in this part of the country and postponing having children because after graduation will come the job search and mad dash for tenure. It's about picking which part of my identity I value more. The chronic anxiety and uncertainty I have come to accept in my life is at times debilitating."

Emma Wilson, who is a year away from earning a PhD in applied linguistics, says that she's already fretting over whether her PhD program is a waste. "This is my big issue. Because of the challenges of obtaining a job in academia, I may not get one. And what if the job I find doesn't require a PhD? Was everything just a waste? I used to feel it wouldn't be, that at least I'd make more money with a PhD, and that education is never a waste because it makes you a better person," she says. "But I've been so traumatized by my experience that I'm not a better person, and in my moments of extreme pessimism I think an unrequired PhD doesn't gain me a higher salary; it gets me a rejection because employers can't pay for a degree they don't need."

Know What You're in for

MENTOR: Barry Johnson

AGE: 24

I WISH I'D KNOWN AT 21 THAT "you should talk to the professors you'd be working with to see if their research interests match yours and what they would expect of you."

Barry Johnson had always planned to go to law school. In college, he added a history minor to his biology major, for which he did an independent study project on the controversy surrounding the discovery of the HIV virus. Although he had intended to focus on researching patent disputes, he found himself easily sidetracked by the primary scientific literature, which fascinated him. Once he came to terms with the fact that he was more interested in the scientific research than the "legal rambling," Barry spent hours grilling friends he knew who were in their first year of grad school. He asked them what grad school involved, what he could expect from it, and how it would affect his future. Now that Barry is in his third year of a PhD program in biology that usually takes about six years to complete, he is watching his classmates drop like flies. "There have been at least eight people who started in my department alone who said that they went to grad school simply because they didn't want to start working yet and weren't sure if they wanted to stay in science. Some talked about going back to do an MBA, another left after two years without a degree and went on to dental school, and another wants to stick around long enough to finish a PhD in biology only to quit science and open a restaurant," Barry says.

Barry can understand the high turnover. He takes two classes per semester in addition to spending fifty hours a week in the lab, and spends more time on those two classes than he did on five classes a semester in college. "I love what I'm doing, but it's a schedule that really burns out those who don't go into it wholeheartedly. But I knew to expect that because I had done my homework beforehand," he says. "I don't think people should go to grad school unless it's for something they are sure they want to do in the future. My advice to anyone considering grad school, but unsure about their desire to pursue a career in that field in the future, would be to find a short-term job in that field after college, maybe for a year or two. Learn what the people who went to grad school do, and try to imagine how you would feel spending the next few decades in that position. If you decide you want to pursue it, the experience will give you a head start when entering grad school and will probably help get you into a more competitive program."

Grad School Is a Goal, Not an Excuse

MENTOR: Tom Hammond
AGE: 31
I WISH I'D KNOWN AT 27 THAT "sometimes the easy or most obvious answer isn't the answer that makes the most sense at the end of the day."

In the first *Quarterlife Crisis*, Tom Hammond shared his story about how he failed at his job in the U.S. Navy's nuclear power program. He was able to use his failure to motivate him to do better in his subsequent jobs, but in 2001 he was stuck in a job and a life that were merely okay. As a civilian defense contractor for the military, Tom liked the people he worked with but wasn't happy with where he saw himself in five or ten years if he stayed in that field. Ever since he graduated from college, Tom had an inkling that he might like to work in higher education. But for five years he had ignored it, and in his defense contractor position, he continued to ignore it for three more years. "When I got out of college, I owed my time to the Navy, so that decision was made for me. Then when I got out, I told myself if I wasn't able to find a job by the fall, I'd look at my options and consider graduate school. It turned out to be easy to find the defense job because I still had the security clearance and the contacts in Washington. It wasn't necessarily the easy way out, but it was convenient. So I thought at least I could make sure that being a defense contractor wasn't what I wanted to do. I struggled the entire three years wondering whether to go to graduate school," Tom says.

Tom wrestled with the idea of going to graduate school in a field he knew he was interested in for several reasons. First, he was hesitant to give up the convenience of already having a good job and the training and security clearance he had earned in the process of getting there. "I was doing what I thought I was supposed to be doing. I didn't know computer science majors who went into the field of higher education. And there were financial aspects. Because I was heading in a totally different direction in my life, my decision didn't sit as well with my parents, who were concerned that I would be giving up a better paying job to make this transition. I knew I wouldn't make the money I'd made two years before, so it took some time to get all right with that," Tom says.

After several years, Tom finally applied to graduate school to pursue a master's degree in higher education and student affairs. This degree will equip him to work with college students in a nonacademic setting, focusing on their development and helping them find out what they want to do with their lives, essentially to ease them through their Quarterlife Crisis. "When I visited the campus for an interview, I just felt like I was meant to be at that school, working with those people, doing that kind of work. Sometimes when you have a feeling about something already and you're put in a situation where that can become a reality, then you can know for sure whether you want to be there. I knew then it was exactly the right decision to make. It also helped knowing I was going to school for the right reasons because I wasn't totally unsatisfied with my job; I just knew there was a better place for me somewhere else in the world. I know people who get unhappy, find something new, get unhappy, find something new. Because I wasn't that unhappy, I knew I had found what I really wanted to do. Grad school wasn't an excuse to get out of something I wasn't enjoying," he says.

One of the most important things Tom learned about the process of going through his 20s is that, in some cases, a length of time is necessary to choose the best path. "Had I worried myself over why I hadn't arrived here as a younger twentysomething, I might never have made it here at all. Eventually, everything clicked into place, and I knew what I needed to do to make myself happy and to fulfill a useful purpose," Tom says. "If you're reading this book and trying to make sense of your own life, taking comfort in the stories of others who are asking themselves the same hard questions you are, and thinking those decisions are a little less daunting now than they were on page 1, then you're already on the right track. I'm sure I'll still struggle, fail, and get overwhelmed from time to time. Because those setbacks are occurring in the positive environment that I now have as my frame of reference, I feel like I'm better equipped to emerge and move on, knowing I'm doing what I'm meant to be doing."

Tom suggests that twentysomethings considering graduate school try a two-step process to help them decide what's best:

Be honest about your motives. Think about your reasons to go back to school and make sure you're doing it for the right ones, *not* because what you're doing now isn't working out and grad school seems like a good alternative.

Get your feet wet. If it's not too time-consuming or expensive, put yourself in a position where you can experience the program. Do an interview or go for a campus visit. "The first time I went up,

I talked to the director of the graduate studies office, and even just that gave me a good feeling," Tom says. "Something that informal might push you to know if that's the right direction or not."

School Is More Than Academics

MENTOR: Susan Goldstein

AGE: 28

I WISH I'D KNOWN AT 25 THAT "a few years ahead, everything you're learning is going to become so valuable, even the small things."

In the first *Quarterlife Crisis* book, "Meredith," whose real name is Susan Goldstein, was grappling with the issue of a high-powered consulting job that left her feeling empty. "Do I make a lot of money? Pretty much. Do I have meetings with CEOs and COOs and other VIPs? Sure do," she said back then. "Am I fulfilled? Not at all. . . . Any time I let myself think [about it], I literally started to shake." When I spoke with her then, she had just left her job and began graduate school at Harvard for a master's in education at a time when the economy was booming.

But by the time she graduated, the HR job market was barren. Susan spent several months making a living by dog sitting and doing some freelance technical research, and seriously questioning whether school was a waste. "In that time, I also became a one-woman networker extraordinaire. I think I met anyone and everyone in the organizational behavior/development field in the greater Boston area. Through this networking and actually through my boyfriend, I met a woman who is a true leader in the field. She and I got along famously from the get-go."

Although the woman's company didn't have an opening, Susan continued to keep in touch with her for several months. And then, because of her graduate school training, the organization created a job specifically for Susan. As the Organizational Development Manager for the Northeast's largest assisted-living company, Susan's "dream job," she works with a team that provides executive coaching and runs a leadership institute for clientele. "I realized then that school was invaluable even if just for the networking opportunities and informational interviews that were expected of students. School wasn't a waste because even when I was dog sitting, I was using my networking skills. Everything I was doing was worthwhile. In the end, school will put you ahead, regardless of the job you get and the economy you graduate in. This is especially true if you study something you feel passionate about and want to make a career out of."

More Ways to Conquer

Beginning with the "What if school was a waste?" question, let's clear up one misconception right away: school does not prepare us for the real world. School is a setting in which we learn things that we might or might not use after we leave the academic environment. There is rarely a short, straight line from School to Career, with the exception of vocational schools. For some reason, we're expected to jump from school to life almost immediately, as if sheltered years in an academic setting somehow equip us to make life decisions that have nothing to do with academics.

Perhaps the most productive way to deal with this question is to accept that although school doesn't prepare us for real-life decision making, it does encompass much more than merely academics. An education is broader than classes. The people you meet, the decisions you make, the lifestyles you learn, the experiences you are exposed to, the revelations you have about what you do and don't like—these all shape who you are. This is why embarking on a career that has nothing to do with your major doesn't mean that choosing that major was a waste. If you hadn't taken that film class, for instance, you wouldn't have met the professor who introduced you to Ethiopian food. If you hadn't slacked off during final exam study period, you wouldn't have realized that you can perform miraculous things at the last minute by pulling all-nighters fueled by Turkish coffee. If you hadn't been at that party, you wouldn't have met the person who is now one of your closest friends.

No experience is a waste, unless you refuse to learn something from it. Learning what you don't want to do at least narrows down the multitude of endless options that can seem so daunting. Figuring out what you don't like is just as important as figuring out what you do.

Another idea to help cope with this issue is to consider that simply because you can't get or don't want a job in a field that follows naturally from your education doesn't mean you won't be able to use those skills in a seemingly unrelated field.

For the question on whether to go to grad school, Barry and Tom offer clear advice and prescribe manageable steps to take to help determine whether you should apply. I would, however, repeat one strong note of caution: if you are considering going to graduate school as a stall tactic, simply because you don't know what else to do, then don't. At the very least, find a job, however menial, in the field you would study before you go ahead and apply. The most common reason twentysomethings I've met have given for regretting going to graduate school is that they only went because they couldn't think of anything better to do. It's imperative to be able to envision yourself doing something several years from now that naturally follows the area of graduate school study you're contemplating. As Trey Sampson, a mentor in this book for other questions, says, "You know you should go to graduate school when you have a plan for exactly what you want to get out of it and what you want to do after you finish. Going into graduate school without a five- to ten-year agenda is like rafting the Colorado River without a paddle."

Part 4

Home, Friends, and Family

As the stresses and concerns of daily life whir around us, our home is supposed to be our refuge, the place where we can escape. When something is going wrong in our lives, it's usually a relief to be able to come home, where we can plunk down somewhere and try to forget about life outside those four walls. How many of us have counted the hours at a job until we could go home, saved our tears from a bad breakup until we closed our door behind us, or slammed down our phone after an argument and found a quiet place to stew?

But what if you can't look forward to the home you come back to? Sometimes conditions at home, such as less than ideal roommates, parental pressures, and geographic location, add to our stress rather than alleviate it. Sometimes home itself is the problem. If your home life is off kilter, it can feel like you're adrift, trying to cling to whatever else in your life seems more dependable. Those are the times when you spend nights at your girlfriend's or boyfriend's place just to get away from your own, work late into the night to dodge your roommates, or stay out drinking and crash on friends' couches to avoid your parents' disapproval.

Home is the place you depend on for a good night's sleep or the place where you lie awake at night, mercilessly pelting yourself with the kinds of Quarterlife Crisis questions found throughout this book. The advice in this section is intended to help you turn your home into the refuge of solace and support you need it to be.

Futhermore, as much as this book is about sifting through our pressures and influences to figure out the identity pulsing beneath the layers, we're not isolated beings. We are profoundly affected by the company we keep. In our 20s, especially, as we form our directions and desires, we feed off each other, competing, comparing, and cheering each other on.

Have you noticed that in certain groups of friends, nearly the entire group seems to get married or want to get married at the same time, go to graduate school, or get a pet? When we don't trust ourselves to make the right decisions, we tend to adopt those of our friends.

Because this tendency is inevitable, if unadvisable, the kinds of people with whom we surround ourselves play a crucial role in how we shape our identities. The ways we socialize have the power to help us build the networks and relationships that can improve our lives or mount the pressures that bring us down. The trick, then, is how to balance maintaining our individuality with the nudges and tugs from other people. The mentors in this section, in their answers to a variety of questions about these relationships, teach us how to do that.

Chapter 15

Why is it so hard to live alone?

Kelly Mcleskey, a 2000 graduate of California State University, Sacramento, says she has fallen into "a funk" recently because she's having a difficult time living alone. "It's hard because I'm at that point in my life where I've done the college thing and settled into my career. But I come home at night, and I'm all by myself. There's no one to share my home with or to share my accomplishments during the day or my bad moments with. I don't have someone home for me to talk to. There's no one to share meals with, and I love cooking. It's hard to do cooking for one because they don't have a grocery store for single people. I'll have good intentions, but the groceries are so big that they spoil by the time I get to them," Kelly says. "It feels kind of empty, very quiet. I have a cat who I talk to all the time, but last night I was just crying, lying on the couch all by myself and asking the cat, 'What should I do?' and the cat doesn't care! It's really bothered me recently. I have too much time to think, so I think too much about my life. I'm usually very happy-go-lucky, but now I've hit bottom."

Make Your Home Your Own

MENTOR: Raquel Aviva

AGE: 32

I WISH I'D KNOWN AT 27 THAT "there is a light at the end of the tunnel. You don't always have to count on others. Work on counting on yourself."

When Raquel Aviva and her boyfriend of five years broke up, he moved out of her apartment, and she found herself at 27 living alone for the first time in her life. She hated it. "I cried, I was depressed, I felt empty, horrible. I had this overwhelming feeling of *being* alone, even though I was close to my family and had good friends," she says.

At first she tried to deal with her empty apartment in New York City by leaving it often. She began dating a man in San Francisco who could afford to fly her there to see him. "He was tall, dark, and handsome, and he entered my life when I needed an escape. I needed that knight in shining armor for that moment. When I felt lonely, I figured I could always go to San Francisco. I traveled a lot, trying not to deal," Raquel says. When the relationship ended, Raquel escaped her apartment as frequently as possible to meet up with other people. Because she loathed Sunday nights alone, she started a Sunday night ritual of going to dinner or a movie with her friends. She also spent longer hours at her job.

Gradually, Raquel realized there were things she could do to make her apartment feel less lonely when she was the only one there. She learned to surround herself with things that made her happy—mostly childhood things like records, DVDs, and '80s tracks. "The things I had and loved as a kid gave me comfort in my 20s. I bought them to make me feel secure in the environment. It was a security blanket," she says. As her '80s collection grew, Raquel's friends began to refer to her apartment as "The Museum."

Once her apartment had something of an identity itself, Raquel not only warmed to it, but she embraced it. She grew so involved with the '80s collection she had started in her apartment that she expanded her fascination with the '80s into *Aquatulle,* a magazine that combines music and the '80s, Raquel's favorite things. "I had to create my own opportunities and successes. I'm a doer. I don't like sitting around. God forbid I have time on my hands. I'm so obsessed with this stuff because when I do something, I need to do it the best, so if I was going to collect '80s stuff, I was going to make it the best '80s collection." She threw herself into her magazine. Eventually, Raquel's apartment became so legendary as a mecca for '80s memorabilia that it received recent press attention in the *New York Times* and *Time Out New York*.

Meanwhile, Raquel learned to be comfortable in solitude. "I had to learn how to live on my own, really and truly. I realized once I was alone that I had leaned on my boyfriend and my parents for support mentally," she says. "I always hated being alone. But going through that process made me okay with it. Only recently have I become okay with being in my apartment by myself. Now I really enjoy solitude sometimes."

Establish Roots

MENTOR: Elizabeth Stern
AGE: 32
I WISH I'D KNOWN AT 29 THAT "you shouldn't set up your place as if it is temporary."

When Elizabeth Stern moved into a studio to live without roommates for the first time in her life, she wondered if she would ever get accustomed to living alone. She had a particularly difficult time getting used to the silence and eating alone. "The initial adjustment period was much longer than I had anticipated. Some of my challenges included not having any socialization unless you pick up the telephone (I spent a lot of time on the phone that first year especially) and being totally dependent on yourself for *everything,* including food and toilet paper, so if you're forgetful or irresponsible, you may realize you have nothing to eat and nothing to wipe yourself with!"

Now, three years after her move, Elizabeth says, "I'm pleased to say that I'm so happy living alone, I don't know if I could ever go back to living with someone. As much as it can get lonely at times, I've figured out some tips that really seem to help."

Fill the void. "Silence can remind you of just how alone you are, so always have some kind of music on, and since it's your place, you get to choose what you are in the mood for (but upbeat music definitely will help to cheer you up if you are lonely). Talking on the phone a lot helped me adjust, as did listening to radio and TV while doing other things."

Invite people to relax. "Don't be afraid to invite people over just to chill or watch TV; they won't think you're desperate."

Embrace solitude. "Don't be afraid of being alone. It can be a relaxing break from the chaos of the outside world and give you a good excuse to reflect and be selfish."

Pretend it's permanent. "Don't set up your place as if it's temporary. Spend the extra $15 to get a bath mat you really like, and get new dishes if you can afford them. It makes a big difference psychologically to be surrounded by things *you* like, not just hand-me-downs from relatives. It will feel more like *your* place, and you will notice. Also, it's flattering to have people over and have them complement your place, saying things like, 'It's so you!' instead of thinking, 'It's so your mother's attic!' "

Don't Be Afraid to Fly Solo

MENTOR: Liz Warner
AGE: 26
I WISH I'D KNOWN AT 20 THAT "you need to do things on your own in order to grow."

When Liz Warner, a 26-year-old from Montana, first began living on her own, she found that the most difficult part of the situation was getting used to the idea that she had to do things by herself. "I had to create my own life, which was very difficult at times," she says. Most of her work colleagues were older with kids at home, and the only people she knew in town were a much older aunt and uncle. "Finally I realized that it wasn't their responsibility to help me make friends. I had to do it myself! I remember one Friday night when I was feeling like an ultra loser and sorry for myself because I didn't have any plans for the weekend, as usual. I really wanted to see this movie, and I finally decided to just go see it by myself. It sounds ridiculous, but it took a lot of guts for me. This whole revelation of 'I can go places by myself' was huge."

Now Liz says that it was worth living alone, especially because of the things she learned about herself and the confidence she was able to build. "I've learned first of all that I'm sociable and I need to talk to people. I think I've actually been depressed some days because I didn't have anyone to talk to and share life with. It has also made me a master mingler conversationalist. Recently I attended a somewhat highbrow party where I only knew three people. I went by myself, something I would have never done in my early 20s. Because of my experiences being alone and dealing with things on my own, I wasn't afraid to mingle and talk to other people at the party. As I went from group to group and met a ton of interesting people, the three people I knew just stared at me in shock. And when I returned to them, they were like, 'You are *so* working this room!' "

Liz also advises the newly roommateless to be patient. "It takes time to get to know people and for them to get to know you. I think you also have to make a pretty big effort to try and meet people. If you're sitting around moping because you're lonely, the only thing you can do about it is go out and meet people. As for the advice I'd give concerning living by yourself, there's also that issue of talking to yourself a lot, so I recommend getting a pet so that all the 'outer monologue' is somewhat legit!"

More Ways to Conquer

Perhaps the main message the mentors in this section illustrate is that living alone isn't the same as being alone. You happen to spend evenings and part of your days in an apartment or house in which you are the only occupant. It's worth reminding yourself that living on your own does not reflect any personal shortcomings. Either you have chosen to live without roommates, or circumstances have forced you to live without roommates temporarily (temporarily because you can always find a roommate if you really want one).

Maybe living alone is difficult for you because you've never been isolated from other people before. Maybe you're afraid of your own company. If you're someone who rarely, if ever, goes to restaurants alone, living alone can seem like hermitude. But it's never too soon or too late to learn to like your own company. After all, you are the only person with whom you're guaranteed to spend the rest of your life.

All three of the mentors suggest that the best way to get used to living alone is to make your place seem familiar. If you make it feel like a home—your home—then the familiarity might come to feel like as much a part of your life as would a roommate. In fact, you might look at this new situation as a blessing: with all of the mentors' advice throughout this book that it's imperative that you "listen to yourself," "find a quiet place," and "sit still," this scenario is the perfect place to comply. Getting to know yourself alone will help you to better define your identity and figure out the things you truly want in life outside of pressures, standards, and other people's expectations.

Chapter 16

What if I feel like I'm "stuck"?

Christina Little, a 24-year-old graduate of Louisiana State University, has been living alone in a Dallas apartment for two years. Her lease was up a year ago, but stuck in a rut of indecision, Christina has been living on a month-to-month lease because she cannot decide on her next step. "Do I renew my lease at my existing apartment, move to another apartment in Dallas, or to a completely different city? Let's hope that by the time this book hits the stores, I'll have made a decision about where to live," she says. "Deep down, I desire to move to a different town that's more comfortable to me, but finding a job in that particular place is out of my control. I feel fresh out of college and have less than two years of job experience in my field. It's frustrating to be stuck in a city I don't fit into, all the while searching unsuccessfully for another job in another town. My fear is that at some point if I don't make decisions, life will make them for me."

Nina O'Connell, a 24-year-old in Michigan, feels the same way. "I feel stuck. I have lived at home and gone to college for the past six years and continue to do so even though I have a full-time job and my undergraduate degree. I have so much debt from school, and as a high school teacher I continue to take classes toward my master's degree, which is costly. I want to move out, but I feel stuck because financially it's too difficult right now. It's like I want to run forward with everything I've got, but someone or something is pushing me back and not allowing me to move forward."

Make a Plan

MENTOR: Valerie Green
AGE: 27
I WISH I'D KNOWN AT 25 THAT "you aren't powerless to change your situation."

A few months after Valerie Green graduated from college with a broadcast journalism degree, she was thrilled to get an offer to be a television producer. The job was a few hours away from her hometown in Missouri, but she was eager to start a new life in a new place and embark on her career. While she enjoyed the job, she earned only $11,000 in her first nine months. When she learned that in television you have to move around to move up, Valerie applied for jobs across the country and was hired at a station in Austin, Texas. "This was quite a distance from my home state, and I didn't know a single person in Austin. But I loaded up my car and drove there. Within weeks I knew I'd hate the job. I just had that feeling. The job wasn't anything like they said it would be, so I was just sort of stranded, broke, and unhappy in a state where I knew no one, and then the economy tanked. I applied for other jobs, trying desperately to get out of that bad situation. I hated that job so badly that I sobbed on my way to work."

"I lived that way for two years," Valerie says, "My parents probably would have paid for me to rent a truck and go back to St. Louis, but to me that felt like giving up and running back home. My boyfriend tried to help me, but he was at wit's end with my work whining. I complained about it all the time. It was all-consuming. A few friends stopped returning calls, and in hindsight I know it was because I whined all the time. They were sick of listening to me. But no one ever said, 'Valerie, quit whining and do something about it!' which was probably what I needed."

The economic downturn continued to hammer Austin. Workers were laid off weekly, including Valerie's boyfriend, a tech worker who was downsized twice. "We wanted to get married, eventually buy a house, and start a life, and we had to face facts that it just wasn't going to happen in Austin," Valerie says. Two years later, they hit upon a solution. "Neither of us saw it as running away from problems but as taking control of a bad situation. We both made a list of the top five cities we'd want to live in based on jobs, cost of living, and overall atmosphere. Chicago was my number one and his number two, so we started saving." After more than a year of scrimping and saving, they had the money to make the move.

Within a few months after the move, Valerie was able to get a job in public relations, a field she was excited about, and her boyfriend secured a contract job at an ad agency. "Money is still tight, but at least I feel like it has the chance to get better," Valerie says. "Just making a tiny step when you're in this situation makes a world of difference. Taking the leap to change something is always hard but sometimes necessary. I noticed that during most of my Quarterlife Crisis, times were worst when I felt absolutely powerless over what was happening to my career, body, or love life. I'd get extremely depressed. It was only when I took control over one little aspect that everything else would follow and I'd start to feel a little bit better."

Take the First Step

MENTOR: Catherine Franklin
AGE: 31
I WISH I'D KNOWN AT 25 THAT "the only way to feel 'unstuck' is to stop trying to figure everything out at once and concentrate on making a first step, as scary as it might be."

After Catherine Franklin graduated from York College, she moved back to the Washington, D.C. area where she had grown up, even though she had a nagging feeling that she didn't want to live there. "I knew I wasn't where I was supposed to be, but I was too scared to do anything about it," Catherine says. "I would come to New York a lot for work. Most of my friends moved there, and I remember thinking everyone was doing what I wanted to do. On the way home to D.C. I had this feeling like, 'Why am I here? I don't belong here.' When I went to visit New York, it just felt like I was coming home. I remembered that I was always completely taken with New York, ever since my first visit at age 7. Meanwhile, I was getting frustrated with living in D.C., which got me pissed off at other things in my life. But I still didn't leave. I was always making excuses why it was never the right time to move to New York: I just got promoted, I just bought new furniture, I'd have to sell my car, I didn't have the money."

Six years later, Catherine found out that her apartment building was going to be torn down and she would be handed relocation money. Suddenly, none of her excuses applied anymore. "That finally unstuck me. I just had to suck it up and do it. I sold my car and got rid of the things I couldn't take to New York. My first day in the city I was like, 'Why didn't I do this five years ago?' We all have our own inner homing device. When you find yourself attached to a certain place, it's like a built-in GPS system. Something in the brain clicks when you know where you're supposed to be. Everything else fell into place—my job, lifestyle, people, culture, activities—all of the things I thought I was lacking in my life. For instance, I had danced since childhood, and in DC there was no outlet for that, but in New York there was. Moving to New York caused a major metamorphosis in my life, personally and professionally."

Catherine's advice for twentysomethings who feel stuck geographically is to ask themselves this question: "If money and fear were not in the equation, where would you be in your life?" She explains, "Fears and apprehension are why people do things for the wrong reasons. If you follow the thread of what you like and where you want to be, money and self-support will follow. I do believe that. There's a quote I read years ago that says, 'You cannot discover new oceans unless you have the courage to lose sight of the shore.' This really resonated with me because I've learned that once you make that first (and often most drastic) step in changing your life in a way that you think will make you happier, the other pieces will fall into place. You just have to be willing to take that first leap. It gets easier from there."

More Ways to Conquer

The mentors who were able to get "unstuck" mentioned one important strategy, an MO that we often forget when we're overwhelmed with the desire to change something. Take one small step, and you'll be on your way. Soon you'll take another small step, and eventually the small steps will add up to a worthwhile change. This is a good strategy for a period of indecision in any part of your life. As long as you're moving, physically or mentally, you're going to luck into a chance meeting or chance experience that will show you something new. You might meet someone who will play some role in your life, or you might learn a skill or activity. You might find a passion by accident. If you're not moving, you learn nothing. So just go. Try. Even the act of trying may make you feel better about yourself. Trying is far better than wallowing or waiting. Because even if you don't move in the exact direction that you thought you would, trying means you're at least moving *somewhere*. Moving somewhere will lead to something, whether it's what you expected or not.

Even if you start by taking the tiniest step, at least you're moving. Brady Muth, a 26-year-old Yankton, South Dakota, native who gives more advice in a later chapter in this book, explains this strategy. "From my experience, I think, don't move on; just keep moving. I don't ever want to move on, or away from, what I have encountered in my life. I don't want to move on, but I also don't want to stand still and get stuck. I always want to keep moving," Brady says. "I had a football coach in college who said you never stay the same. You always move forward or you move backward, but you never stand still. So I guess I look at it from the perspective that I always want to move forward and grow, but my experiences have shaped who and what I am, and I never want to forget that."

Chapter 17

Why is it so hard to find friends?

Pamela Schwedler, a 24-year-old in Boston, has asked herself this question many times since she moved from the Midwest to the East Coast. "I had lived in Michigan my entire life and was ready to explore. I wanted to expand my worldview, live somewhere different, and meet new people. I didn't know anyone in the area I was moving to, but I figured I'd surely be able to make new friends as I had in college. I got a job, found some people to move in with, and was on my way. I met some people my age at work, but they weren't people I wanted to hang out with. When the roommate thing didn't work out, I got an apartment by myself, which was fine with me. But I really wasn't making any friends," she says.

Pamela tried taking a graduate class to meet people, but her classmates didn't socialize during class and went straight home afterward. "I wasn't going to take a pottery class or something just to meet people, because I'm not interested in that stuff. It's not like you go out to bars and meet people to be friends with, if you even have anyone to go out with in the first place. I met plenty of guys to date if I wanted to, but I never met any girls to become friends with. I've begun to feel like I'm asking girls out on dates, like, 'Um . . . you want to hang out sometime?' It's been really hard, and after more than two years, though I do still have my friends who live in other states, I still don't have any girlfriends here."

Become the Ringleader

MENTOR: Andrea Davis
AGE: 27
I WISH I'D KNOWN AT 22 THAT "people will respond to what they think they see in you and the confidence level and image you project."

When Andrea Davis moved to New York City after college, she expected that because she had attended school in Connecticut, she would naturally know people in New York. "Surprise, surprise, none of my close friends moved to New York," she says. "I spent my first few months going to visit my boyfriend, who was still in college, because I was so lonely. I kept returning to my boyfriend and the safety of that environment every weekend instead of going for it in New York. Then when we broke up, I hadn't built up a support network and I was alone. I remember my main feelings were, 'Why am I such a loser? Why can't I meet people and everyone else seems to be able to? Why is it so much harder for me? Have I lost my touch?' I began to doubt I was saying anything interesting and wondered, 'Am I just a boring person?' It was awful."

Now Andrea says she has a "concrete" suggestion for how to meet friends that worked for her as soon as she tried it, and it has worked again several times since. "It was advice from my mother, and it worked perfectly. The secret is to create events, invite people to them, and then even if they can't make it, they'll think of you as 'someone who has things going on' and might just invite you to their next event," Andrea says. "For instance, tell someone you work with, 'A bunch of us are going to get drinks next week sometime,' and then tell a couple other someones that same thing. Or 'We're going to a movie this weekend if you're interested.' No one has to know that there's no 'we' besides you; all it takes is a couple people to say yes and you have a 'we.' On the outside chance only one person says yes, it's as simple as, 'My friend's swamped with work at the last minute. Oh well, you and I can grab a drink and I'll introduce you guys next time.' Any party invite I got, I passed on to ten others—you never know when someone (like I was) is feeling undersocial and will jump at the chance to meet new people. I joined two clubs on *www.craigslist.org,* one that goes to a movie once a month and one that sees local bands. Anybody can start up a club like that, and nobody expects you to bring someone. Seriously, the trick for me was to not be intimidated by my own loneliness. Creating energy and activity and fun around me made others want to be part of that excitement."

Beyond the group forming, Andrea says it is important for twentysomethings to understand that the image we project relates directly to how easily we can find friends. "When you leave school, you go through a major change of life. There you had a pattern, a culture, and a network, and you were safe and secure. It's understandable and natural to wonder why you can't just jump into your new life with your running shoes on and go full speed ahead. It doesn't work like that for anybody," she says. "You do start to wonder after a time, *Why can't I seem to get this to work for me?* Well, if you project the image that you're alone and miserable, people naturally are not going to be drawn to that. They will be drawn to someone who looks upbeat and like she has things going on. So something I did was I'd say to myself that I was going to pretend I was having a good day. I made it my goal for the day to look happy even though I wasn't. Not only did people gravitate toward me, but somehow the day ended up better."

Restructure for Opportunities

MENTOR: Trey Sampson
AGE: 34
I WISH I'D KNOWN AT 25 THAT "if you get involved in things, it's easy to keep up momentum, but once you stop, it's hard to start again. Seize the initiative early on."

Finding friends was, for Trey Sampson, the "big challenge" of his 20s. Although he was shy throughout his childhood and adolescence, he spent enough time in structured environments like school and sports teams to break up moments of isolation. "They also provided a ready channel for casual-time activities. If you didn't have anything to do on Friday, you called up members of your team or the guys you hung out with during lunch to organize something interesting. College took this situation to the extreme. My freshman dorm was sort of like a proxy family," Trey says. "Grad school was different. You become a jealous guardian of your personal time. Letting somebody in on that time is a big deal, so unless they're putting out in the sex department, it's better to keep friends and acquaintances at an arm's length."

To make matters worse, all of Trey's college friends had moved away, and Trey began graduate school just as he and his live-in girlfriend broke up. "When the girlfriend disappeared, I found myself suddenly in a personal vacuum of my own construction. Not only was I not getting laid, I also wasn't getting any of the casual chitchat that turns out to be just as important to maintain a positive attitude. Most grad students at school had their own lives (and in some cases, wives) and were hesitant to let somebody with a dark cloud hanging over his head intrude," Trey says. "When I graduated, I realized I was going to be by myself for the first time ever. I briefly considered getting a shared rental with a roommate, but somewhere inside I knew it would be better in the long run if I just sucked it up and moved into a studio. The first winter in that studio was painful. I was living in Oakland, miles from the Berkeley campus and no real friends in the neighborhood. On weekends, I drove a hundred miles to Sacramento to attend house parties or forty miles down to Palo Alto to see my sister still in school. It was the classic California situation where if my car had been totaled, my social life would have evaporated completely."

Trey invested all of his energy into work, hoping that he could make friends through that outlet. But the friends he made weren't the "true" friends he could call at two in the morning in an emergency; they were more like casual work friends who would happily split a pitcher of beer with him on Friday and then part ways until Monday. "For more than two years, there were many weekends, most weekends actually, where I spoke to nobody aside from the occasional call to my parents. During the day, for entertainment, I rode my bike around Berkeley and watched movies alone. At night, I went to a bookstore or bar, keeping to myself. At one point, about two years after grad school, I realized I'd only been to one party per year since graduation."

At around that time, Trey hit a turning point where he was able to accept that being alone forced him to be comfortable with his own company. "I didn't like being alone during this period, but I realized that my ability to stay sane even while spending so much time outside of direct human company was a good sign. I wasn't a freak. I wasn't an ogre. I was just painfully shy and lacking the tools or insight to meet new people," he says. "But I also knew I needed to break out. The opportunities were there, but the inertia was high. The two potential avenues for socialization that intrigued me the most were soccer and swing dancing. I eventually chose soccer, mainly because I wanted to get in shape. I got put on a team with a bunch of other 'independent' players, and we quickly bonded. Suddenly, I was going to parties and even dating again. Granted, I still found myself spending a lot of time waiting uncomfortably for the phone to ring, but the realization that things could turn around so quickly helped. Since then, whenever I've felt lonely or stagnant, I start looking for some place to sign up for dance lessons, language lessons, volunteer activities—whatever."

Having dealt for so many years with the question of finding friends, Trey wants to offer words of wisdom to twentysomethings in the same situation he was in. "Speaking from the perspective of a now-married thirtysomething, I feel I have an obligation to those following in my footsteps. The one thing you have to realize about adult friendships is that they aren't like childhood or collegiate friendships. Crashing on somebody's couch after a night of drinking gets a little pathetic past your 25th year. By the same token, the number of opportunities to sit under the stars and wax philosophic about the universe with a person who isn't looking to be your life partner starts to decline around the same time. Adults have rigid emotional boundaries," Trey says. "So here's what it boils down to: maybe the reason you can't find friends is because you lack the structured situations and chance mechanisms that introduced you to past friends. If so, you can easily restructure your life to get back into such situations. It's basically a matter of overcoming inertia. Still, it helps to accept the changing dynamics of friendship as you get older and to learn to be comfortable with the occasional periods of isolation that occur in any active adult life."

More Ways to Conquer

Trey explained the answer to this question clearly and concisely: "It's basically a matter of overcoming inertia." Finding new friends takes courage and creativity, but most of all it takes action. How can you meet people if you're spending most of your time at home feeling sorry for yourself because you aren't meeting people? So many of us immerse ourselves in reality TV or the Sims games, where we watch other people have lives instead of working on our own. We're a generation perhaps more comfortable with the safe but inexpressive communication through a computer than we are with face-to-face encounters. If you want to find new friends, it might help to force yourself to turn off the TV, to call people instead of IMing them.

This is not to say that finding friends is easy, which leads to my next point. It may be helpful to assure yourself that few twentysomethings enter young adulthood armed with a ready-made posse. Friends scatter after graduation, and relationships formed in school often dwindle. It can take years to build new friendships, especially to form a cohesive group rather than friends here and there who don't know each other. So don't beat yourself up if you haven't yet solidified friendships in your area. The mentors' suggestions in this section should give you a head start, especially Andrea's tried-and-true method of finding friends. Invite people to do things. As Pamela feared, making new friends *is* practically like asking people on dates. But the sting of rejection shouldn't be as great; if someone doesn't want to hang out with you, then you don't want to be that person's friend, anyway. Because there's less to lose, you can treat scenarios more casually than dating.

Maura, a 31-year-old from the first *Quarterlife Crisis*, shared for that book how it took her eighteen months to find a friend when she first moved to New York from the Midwest, and she beat herself up because of it. She now counsels patience. "Moving to a new city is so hard; I deserved some sympathy for that. But it was ridiculous for me to think I would never have a friend again. I treated it like dating; I was trying too hard to find friends. Once I backed off, it happened more naturally. I just needed to give myself time and patience and get to know people. Looking back, I could have gone online to find people, too," she says.

Many of the twentysomethings I've interviewed had the greatest and quickest success with building friendships by joining groups. Soccer teammates become gym buddies. Company softball teammates become happy hour partners. Theater groups become dinner-and-movie friends. Fellow volunteers become pizza-and-beer partygoers. Come up with a few activities that you're interested in, and then join an organization related to those activities, and if you don't click with the people involved, leave and join another group or team. Finally, when someone asks you to do something, even if you don't really feel like getting up off the couch to go do it, consider going anyway. You never know when someone will introduce you to your next best friend.

Chapter 18

What if my friends and I are drifting apart?

"This is a big problem for me, and unfortunately, I don't know what to do about it, really," says Jenny Harris, a 23-year-old in a Chicago suburb. "My best friend since high school and I recently stopped talking to each other. I feel really awful about it, but I also don't feel up to talking to her anymore. It definitely feels like we're just going in different directions, and that maybe there's nothing I can do to change that."

Jenny attributes the drift to the divergent paths she and her friend took in their 20s. Jenny went to graduate school immediately after college, while her friend, who worked for a few years after high school, is now halfheartedly pursuing an undergraduate degree while working part-time jobs in a café and a movie theater. "I don't care whether she goes to school, but I think it changes you in some ways, and *that's* the real issue," Jenny says. "We have different attitudes about work, careers, responsibility. She calls me to go out drinking all the time. Admittedly I used to be a big partier, and reveled with her in being ridiculously irresponsible and spontaneous, but I can't act like that anymore. I have work to do every night, and I have to be in class in the morning; it's not like college, where you can blow off class. She often stays out drinking and either goes to work hungover or late. Her attitude is if she loses her job, so be it; she'll find another. I'm working on something bigger, and I'm not about to jeopardize that by goofing off all the time. I've tried explaining that it's nothing personal, that I just have things I have to do at night and have to be up in the morning, but she constantly gives me crap about it and gets pissed off when I don't go out. I feel bad turning my back on ten years of friendship and walking away, but I also feel like we have very different lifestyles and are heading in different directions, and maybe this is just how it goes. I honestly feel like we've drifted so far apart that maybe there's just nothing left to save."

Your History Can Be Your Common Ground

MENTOR: Leia Gardner

AGE: 24

I WISH I'D KNOWN AT 22 THAT "time and distance don't have to kill bonds with friends."

Like Bailey, Leia Gardner started drifting from her best friend from childhood when in her 20s her and her best friend's paths took markedly different directions. Even when they lived in the same town, the friendship wasn't easy to sustain. Leia became involved with a church group, moved in with girls she met there, and concentrated on stoking the new friendships. "I think I devoted too much time to satisfying that group of friends, and dating a lot of the guys of whom my friend never approved (rightly so, in hindsight). Plus, my friend was in another phase of life—she was about to get married. Even though we lived in the same town, we rarely saw each other, and I think we would both admit it was for selfish reasons. When we first started to drift, I felt mostly resentment. I believed she felt she was too good for me, and I think she probably was feeling the same thing. I felt I didn't know her and I couldn't relate to her anymore. I could see her changing, but it was without me." When Leia's friend and her new husband moved to a town several hours away, their occasional visits seemed strained.

In the fall of 2002, Leia happened to call her friend just hours after a tragic death in the friend's family. Leia knew she would drive to the funeral, but wasn't sure if her friend would want her to come sooner. "I called her sister and asked if she would want me there, and her sister told me to get my butt over there," Leia says. "A lot of things happened in her life after that tragedy. That weekend, I saw the girl I had grown up with really show her maturity. She was so strong for her family, and I had overwhelming pride for her. And I think we realized then how much we needed each other. In the weeks to follow, we talked every day and told each other, 'I love you,' before we got off the phone, which we never did in our whole ten-year friendship. Now we visit more often. I also think I realized that just because we live different lives doesn't mean we don't have anything in common. We have such a rich history together, and she's more like a sister than a friend."

Leia's advice to twentysomethings who may want to salvage a drifting friendship sounds natural but is something many twentysomethings tend to overlook or fear. "I think the biggest mistake she and I made was that we didn't talk about our drifting, and if we did, it was in a cowardly manner, via e-mail. If it weren't for the tragic circumstances, I might have never gotten to have this terrific level of intimacy that I now have with my best friend," Leia says. "And another thing is to realize that someone you love doesn't have to have tons in common with you. We don't have lots in common anymore, but we talk about everything anyway. Plus, we enjoy talking about the old times, silly things we did in school. I learned that when a friend gets married or is in another stage of life than you, it requires lots of effort to keep up. But I could never just let go of a friend who I can't ever remember not having, just because her life is a little different from mine."

Relationships Will Change

MENTOR: Brian Weiner

AGE: 24

I WISH I'D KNOWN AT 22 THAT "it's okay that I don't routinely keep in touch with every friend from college and that they don't keep in touch routinely either.

"This was the question I most struggled with, particularly after my first year of college," says Brian Weiner, a 2002 graduate of Muhlenberg College. "By our early 20s, the high school drinking friends have all had their share of experiences, and home reunions at bars become anecdotes of who had the worse drinking experience. After a while, you just want to say, 'I know! Enough already! Can we move on?!' "

After a few months of these mini-reunions, Brian says it becomes increasingly difficult to sustain friendships on the basis of reliving past antics. As twentysomethings' lives get busier and they focus more on careers, casual bar-scene friendships dwindle. "Friendships become fewer but more meaningful. In high school you have twenty-five friends, in college fifteen, and postcollege maybe three or four. You have to start questioning the importance and value of another's friendship, I think," Brian says.

Recently, Brian decided to move into a small apartment with his best friend so that they could better keep up their friendship. "Though we both have our own rooms, we still feel occasional tension, much more now that we live together. At one point we even began feeling as if we were competing, because the real world requires both of us to experience life on our own, find new friends, and explore the single life. But although our schedules and lifestyles are different, we've learned to compromise. She's still my best friend, and I wouldn't trade her in for anything in the world. It's both difficult and valuable to love your best friend unconditionally. When we get tense, I try (and it is *so* hard sometimes) to think about what it is about her that makes me laugh. You just have to realize that by age 23, you don't just break a friendship off because of a minute tiff," Brian says. "I would tell twentysome-things to try to patch the friendship. You may have to come to the conclusion that you weren't meant to spend every hour of every day laughing with this person. Schedule a Tuesday night ('MTV lineup night') and dedicate that weekly spot to him or her, as that will distance you enough but keep you in touch over something you have in common."

More Ways to Conquer

We keep people in our lives for various reasons. We might have a few friends we call when we want to go drinking or clubbing, another friend we call when we feel like going for a walk or to the gym, another we hang out with to watch the game, and another whose shoulder we cry on. If we're lucky, we have a few friends with whom we can do all of the above. When we begin to drift from one of these friends, or when our interests seem to diverge, that's not necessarily a cue that it's time to cast the friend from our lives. Instead, at that point you can evaluate the role that friend has played in your life, what role you *want* that friend to play, and whether he or she can continue to play that role. If not, that role can always shift. Cry-on-the-shoulder friends can pull back to be watch-the-game friends. Drifting gym buddies can become once-in-awhile barhoppers. And there's nothing wrong with that.

It can be particularly disheartening when you seem to drift from several friends at once. This is natural in our 20s because it's inevitable that as we move into adulthood, there will be more demands on our time, more priorities that we can't help placing above giving a friend a call. It's also natural to drift from childhood friends because of how we made friends in our youth: the children and teenagers we associated with were most often people with whom we happened to go to school, and the pool of people at our schools was based mostly on geographical location. Whereas adulthood friendships usually begin by noticing common interests, childhood friendships began because of something as random as geographical location; no wonder they can be difficult to sustain. If it seems that you've drifted from several friends at about the same time, it may be helpful to look at how much of an effort you've been able to put into those relationships and whether, as you've been juggling the other aspects of your life, you've unwittingly plunked the friendships near the bottom of your priority list.

If it seems like you and your friends no longer have anything in common, or that your relationships are perhaps now based more on rehashing old times than on enjoying the present, there is something you can try before letting those friendships fade. Create new things to have in common. Start a weekly or monthly ritual, as did Raquel, who in chapter 16 shared how she began a Sunday night tradition to keep up with friends. I've found that many twentysomethings, particularly guys, successfully create a new common bond by participating in fantasy sports leagues with their friends. As they navigate the season, making trades and heckling opponents, they have an easy excuse to stay in touch with friends.

Also, keep in mind that we're likely to stay in touch more frequently when we send brief "Hey, how are you" e-mails than when we write long, story-filled e-mails that might make others feel as if they need to find the time to reciprocate with an equally long and involved answer.

Finally, as you continue through your 20s and 30s, you'll come to realize, if you haven't already, that you aren't expected to keep up with friends as often as you did as a teenager to maintain the friendships. It's perfectly normal to be close friends with someone whom you can manage to see only a few times a year. As long as you can pick up right where you left off, there's no reason to feel guilty when other aspects of life are vying for your time.

Chapter 19

How do I stop comparing myself to other people?

Greg Aarons is a 24-year-old who graduated from Connecticut College after five and a half years. In the bleak employment landscape, he can't afford to move out of the tiny two-bedroom apartment he rents with his divorced father. "I was confident that when I got out of college I'd be able to support myself. I thought I'd get a $30,000-a-year job right away, live in my own apartment, and have a girlfriend," he says. "Instead, I'm single, I live in my father's two-bedroom, I can't find friends, tomorrow I'm interviewing for a job that basically involves cleaning senior citizens' poop, and I think I'm going to take it. In college I might have made fun of kids who cleaned up poop, whereas now it doesn't even seem like that bad a proposition, which is scary."

For Greg, the most difficult aspect of his Quarterlife Crisis is that he feels extra inadequate because he compares himself to other twentysomethings and always believes his life falls short. "It's hard. I compare myself to friends I had in college who seem like they're all living together in the city with decent jobs. Their parents helped them, and my dad can't afford to. They're way ahead of me in life. I'm just trying to survive until my next paycheck while filling out applications for my next job," Greg says.

"And I'm in the shadow of a 27-year-old brother who was an Ivy Leaguer like my father and got two graduate degrees I can't pronounce, while I'm going to clean old people's poop. The irony is like something on a comedy show. It's really depressing. I don't even want to leave the house because I'm so embarrassed about my life."

Comparing Is a Waste

MENTOR: Maura Jones
AGE: 31
I WISH I'D KNOWN AT 27 THAT "like many twentysomethings, I didn't give myself enough credit."

In the first *Quarterlife Crisis*, we met Maura, who constantly compared her life to her peers' and never managed to feel like she measured up. In terms of comparisons, Maura understands exactly where Greg is coming from. "I feel like everyone else is ahead of me, like I'm not where I should be in terms of relationships, friends, jobs," she said back then. "It's a long and painful road."

Four years later, Maura has a thriving social circle, a serious live-in boyfriend, and a powerful career with famous clients in the entertainment industry. "I learned you need to stop comparing yourself to other people as soon as possible because otherwise you can do it forever, and there's always going to be someone who has more than you," she says. "Comparing only makes you miserable, and it's a complete waste of time and energy. Someone else will always have better furniture and clothes, but there will always be someone with more debt than you, too."

The easiest trap for twentysomethings to fall into, Maura says, is to compare themselves financially. But that kind of emphasis can be misleading. "It's a much more complicated question than who makes more money. I have friends whose parents gave them $75,000 for a down payment. I have friends who make loads of money but absolutely dread going to work every day," she says.

"And I'm just starting to learn how much people live above their means to create an appearance. One of my friends gave his wife an incredible diamond ring, but he's $50,000 in credit card debt. Tell yourself not to try to keep up with everyone because you don't necessarily know the real situation."

Maura says she still occasionally struggles with comparing herself to peers, but this time she has learned to put her thoughts in check. Recently, three of her former coworkers, several years younger than she, opened their own company. "At first, when I heard that, I felt awful. I don't have my own company," Maura says. "But then instead of continuing to compare myself, I thought, 'I don't want one.' Just because I can't do that right now doesn't mean I should or I want to. They did something risky and huge that I don't think would be right for me right now. There's no point in feeling bad about it. Comparing myself is never going to make me happy. If you start comparing yourself in your 20s, you're setting yourself up for a pattern for life. You're going to meet people at all different levels. You need to learn to be pleased with yourself."

Over the past four years, Maura has taught herself to focus on her own achievements. Comparing herself to where she was in the past is healthier than scrutinizing the contrast between her life and others'. "I can look back at who I used to compare myself to and see that I now have a lot of the stuff I wanted: I have a bedroom, a sofa, and a savings account. I had thought I was going to be living in a hovel until I was 45. I still have student loans, but no more credit card debt, which is a huge improvement. While my boyfriend and I don't own our apartment, we're doing really well," she says. "I can tell myself now that things are eventually going to work out in my favor. Now that I know everything worked out fine, I realize twentysomethings don't give much credit to themselves. Everything is so dire. But the things we do right out of college, especially our first few jobs, don't matter after a few years. Eventually, they're going to be a distant memory."

Now when Maura catches herself in comparison mode, she uses the opportunity to step back, break down her thoughts, and ask herself three important questions rather than let her feelings of inadequacy fester. For example, when she heard that her younger coworkers founded their own company, she asked herself:

Why is this upsetting? Maura was able to attribute her frustration to her insecurity with her own career path. Because she entered her field in her mid-20s, she felt as if she were already behind peers who joined the field right out of school.

Do I really want what they have? When Maura thought about it objectively, she realized that if she truly wanted to start her own company, she could certainly give it a shot. But that career move didn't make sense for her at that point, and she wasn't positive she even wanted to go off on her own in the first place.

Maura's attitude was different toward her financially well-off friends, the ones who had high-paying jobs or generous parents. When she asked herself if she wanted more cash, the answer, of course, was "Hell, yes." But Maura was able to get over her jealousy (which is what these comparisons ultimately boil down to) by telling herself two things:

- "Some people are privileged. The fact that I am not means I am that much more capable because I have earned my accomplishments."

- "I don't have that much money, but I do have more than I had before, so I am moving in the right direction. If I keep doing what I'm doing, I will have what I want someday."

How can I use these feelings productively? Instead of wasting time wallowing in a state of have-not, Maura now turns her jealousy into a motivating force. They are starting their own company?

Maura will find more clients. They have more money? Maura will work harder. To put it bluntly, these feelings can give her the kick in the ass she needs to jump-start her drive toward her goals.

Once Maura has thought through these issues, she will not allow herself to make the same comparison to the same people again. When she finds herself thinking about the situation, she simply reminds herself that she already made peace with that comparison and forces herself to put it out of her mind.

What's Important Is What *You* Want

MENTOR: David Holmes
AGE: 25

I WISH I'D KNOWN AT 24 THAT "I shouldn't compare myself to other people, but instead should only compare myself to the person whom I want to be."

David Holmes, who grew up in Cranston, Rhode Island, was generally a confident guy until he was 24. He hovered near the top of his class at a well-respected, first-tier law school and worked one summer at a large, prestigious law firm. Almost all of the other summer interns were from schools like Harvard, Yale, and Stanford. "Despite my success in law school, I felt self-conscious to be around my coworkers at times. In the beginning, I was even a little embarrassed to tell these Ivy League stars where I went to school. I'm proud of my education, but I couldn't help but feel inferior while telling some Yale law student who was a Princeton undergrad that my schools weren't Ivy League level. I come from an environment where just telling someone that you go to law school, no matter which one, would impress them. But suddenly I was agonizing over the fact that my law school somehow wasn't as good as others," David says.

David's attitude began to change about halfway through the summer during a walk home from a firm happy hour. He was walking with two coworkers, a Harvard student and a Columbia student, when one of them said, "You know, I think you're one of

the smartest out of all of us, even though you're from that school."
David says, "While he didn't phrase that comment in the most
diplomatic of ways, I knew that he really meant it as a compli-
ment, and it got me thinking. Here I was with all of these Ivy Lea-
guers, and I had the same damn job as all of them. I didn't have go
to schools like Yale to get the job like they did. But this was just
my first step. What allowed me to stop comparing myself to my
peers is when I learned to compare what I am doing only to what
I want to do. I'm doing exactly what I want. Therefore, it
shouldn't matter what others are doing. If I want to work at X law
firm in Y city on Z matters, and that's exactly what I'm doing, it
shouldn't bother me that some coworkers went to 'better' schools.
I'm doing what I want, they're doing what they want, we should
all be happy."

David says his advice to twentysomethings stuck in comparison mode is to "think of what it is you really want, and work hard
to get there. And once you're there, don't worry about what other
people are doing. If you have what you want, that's all that really
matters. If you look hard enough, there's always going to be someone with something 'better.' The home run champion may not
have the highest batting average in the league. But why should that
bother him? He can't be the best at everything. And that's the
point: you're not going to be the best at everything. If you have
what you want, who cares about anyone else?"

More Ways to Conquer

Many of us begin relentlessly comparing ourselves when we're in
school. Someone else might have a more prestigious internship,
for example, or a friend's parents are going to help her with rent,
or a classmate seems to know exactly what she wants to do with
her life and exactly how to get there. Once we shift into the real
world, the comparisons extend beyond jobs to barometers such as
financial status, romantic status, material goods, number of
friends, and social calendars.

The most important point I want to get across to you here is that it is absolutely useless to compare your life to someone else's because the other person's life is probably not quite how it seems to you. People our age work hard to create an impressive appearance when reality maybe isn't so kind. You might notice that your friend has a fabulous designer wardrobe, for example, but you might not know that she also happens to be $20,000 in credit card debt. Or you might meet a guy who makes $100,000 a year and not realize that he dreads going to his sixteen-hour job every morning.

Twentysomethings don't talk about the dark side of twenty-something life. We are tremendously skilled at putting up fronts that make it seem like we have it all together, like our lives are smooth and glamorous. Part of the reason our 20s are great is that we get to create our identity. But one reason these years can be so difficult is that we feel forced to figure out our identity *now*. The ways we build our images often represent the ways we hope to define ourselves, or at least to get some sense of our own direction. So we are often willing to go to great lengths to put up our fa-cades, because the more we can support the image we create, the more we will feel like we're carving out our own identity in the process. What this means is that the people to whom you're comparing yourself most likely have problems and issues beneath what you can see. So to compare yourself to them when you're only aware of the most superficial pieces of their lives isn't fair to yourself. As Teale Dotson, one of the mentors elsewhere in this book, puts it, "Don't feel like you need to 'keep up with the Jone-ses,' because the Joneses are in debt from trying to keep up with the Smiths!"

The mentors in this chapter offer several good suggestions and outlooks to help you work through the issue of comparing, so I'll add only one more tip here: don't focus on what you don't have; focus on what you do. No matter where in your life you seem to fail to "measure up," there are always other parts of your life—a fun group of friends, a great relationship with your parents, an apartment (however tiny) in an ideal location—of which you can be proud. Start with confidence and pride in that small aspect of your life, and work to build out from there.

Chapter 20

Should I move back in with my parents?

"*Hello!* This one is *so* me," says Meg Talbot, who moved in with her parents in New England after she separated from her husband. Because when she recently decided to go to graduate school, she was still married and didn't qualify for financial aid, she had no resources to be able to afford her own apartment. "Luckily, my parents said I could stay with them. I appreciate it, but come on—I'm 30 and shouldn't be living *with my parents*!" she sighs. "I guess it's more accepted now, but still. Do you think I'll be able to bring a guy back to my childhood room and have wild (or even not wild) sex so close to my parents' room? Even if they were okay with it, it would be a total obvious mood kill for me. At least it's more socially acceptable for a woman to move back in with her parents than for a man."

Forget What Society Tells Us

MENTOR: S. Ayleen Edwin
AGE: 25
I WISH I'D KNOWN AT 22 THAT "society standards are silly. There's simply no logic in the idea that we're more successful if we're

living in the miserable reality of a mentally, emotionally, physically, and financially stressful situation, as long as we don't resort to moving home again."

After S. Ayleen Edwin graduated from Arizona State University, she moved back home and, for awhile, felt embarrassed about the stigma of living with her parents. "Society says that when the little chicks get older, it's time to leave the nest. The freeloading birds left behind, therefore, must be little more than lazy worm-gulping branch potatoes. Particularly in moments when I felt I was nowhere near to reaching the goals I set in my earlier youth, I really felt the frustration of living at home. Those were the moments when you stop and think, *Yikes, I can't even support myself, let alone actually become prosperous,*" she says. "But that's just not true. Of course I could support myself. I pay bills at my parents' house and I get along famously with them; besides, because of the strange hours I keep, I'm generally the only one there when I'm actually home. I've come to learn that the birds don't obtain more or better worms just because they aren't in the same nest as their parents. They do, however, seem to catch fewer worms when they are too stressed out to recognize their own reflection in the birdbath. My parents continue to serve as sincere emotional support for me, as I do for them."

Ayleen quotes suffragist Carrie Chapman Catt, who said, "No written law has ever been more binding than unwritten custom supported by popular opinion," and says the statement hit home for her situation. "The truth hurts, but people really do seem to frown on a 25-year-old who lives in her parents' home," Ayleen says. "But despite society's feelings on the subject, I'm here to say they don't know what they're missing. The time I spent on my own was an incredible learning experience and wonderful opportunity for personal growth. But I have a wonderful relationship with my parents; we've built a support structure that would be the envy of any lonely individual. Above all, I have the foresight to know that the time isn't so far away when I will be sitting at a funeral service, grateful even for the few simple nights I spent watching *CSI* with my parents while my sister searches her memory desperately for the most recent moment of happiness in their presence."

They Make Supportive Roommates

MENTOR: Hansel Tomameng

AGE: 33

I WISH I'D KNOWN AT 23 THAT "there are far more important things to enjoy and cherish than to worry about being embarrassed about living with your parents."

If Hansel Tomameng hadn't moved back home after college, he likely wouldn't be where he is today. Because Hansel's parents defied Filipino cultural expectations by supporting him despite his lack of a clear career goal, he felt free to enter a series of jobs after college that weren't financially successful in the eyes of his culture. He interned for the San Francisco Giants for one season at $5 an hour, he wrote copy for an NBC sports affiliate for free, he assistant managed a Champs Sports store for $6 an hour, and he sold shoes at Niketown for less than $10 an hour.

At that point in his life, Hansel began volunteering as a mentor for at-risk youth, an activity he continued for three years before he was able to parlay his experience into a paying job. Now, as a family advocate and care manager for an intensive care agency for the city and county of San Francisco, he says he makes half the publicized salary of a UCLA graduate, but he was recently publicly recognized for being a role model for at-risk youth.

For Hansel, living with his parents and grandmother allowed him to have experiences he couldn't have had if he were on his own in San Francisco. "When I came home, my parents supported my decision to take jobs that did not require a degree because they had faith that I was taking steps towards finding a vocation I would enjoy for a lifetime instead of having to work a job just for money. Because of them, I found my calling," he says. "In hindsight, my parents continued to raise me after 18, where most American children cannot wait to leave home and parents feel a sense of closure. And now, as a result of my success in my career, many other parents have been coming up to my mom and dad to ask how they raised me to be patient with their teenagers."

In the beginning, Hansel was slightly embarrassed to be living with his family, even though he paid rent, utilities, and car insurance. "My main concern was bringing home a lady friend and explaining that I still live with my parents. I avoided this potentially awkward predicament by avoiding my home. As I got older, I saw my parents as roommates and the embarrassment decreased. I have met more people my age still at home and we joke about it more. I have two adult female roommates who at times make me feel like Jack from *Three's Company,* except the Ropers happen to be my parents and my dad is a better super than Mr. Furley."

Hansel says he would tell twentysomethings living with their parents or considering the move to consider how the scenario will benefit them in the long term. "The support will allow you to take advantage of these formative years to build relationships and obtain experience essential for the rest of your life. If you can stomach it for a few years, live with your parents and get them to recall their stories of youth and their young adulthood. By living with them at this stage, you will be able to help discover your strengths and the not-so-good habits you subconsciously acquired as you grew up. Increasing your awareness of the effects your parents had on you will undoubtedly help you fulfill your dreams."

It Makes Financial Sense

MENTOR: Leigh French

AGE: 28

I WISH I'D KNOWN AT 27 THAT "the outcome of my decision to live at home was going to be one of the best decisions I could have made financially for my future."

After living out of state for several years, Leigh French returned home to Charlotte, North Carolina, to move in with her father. "I knew it was the right thing to do for a number of reasons, but mainly because it was a brilliant way to get out of debt. I was frustrated with not being able to have people over and dealing with remarks when people found out I still lived at home. It was annoying. People acted like I was spoiled and supported by my dad, which was far from the case. When I would say I didn't have the money to spend on something, they would say things like, 'You should have a ton of money; you're living off your dad.' It was more the tone than anything," Leigh says. "I felt like I had to explain to anyone who found out I lived at home why I was doing it and how I wasn't taking advantage of or being supported by my dad. It made me feel like a kid, and I was 27."

But Leigh learned quickly that putting up with the nasty comments was worth it in the end. Within a year after she had moved back home, she paid off her car, a line of credit, and a credit card. "I would never be in the financial place I am in life without living with my dad. You have to know that people are going to judge virtually everything you do in life; you just have to do what works for you. In this case, I think the feelings of not being adequate were well worth the payoff," she says. "If you're living with your parents, you should make the best of the situation financially and save, save, save. Enjoy the time you have with your parents, no matter how much they get on your nerves at times, as this is a unique time in your lives together: it's the bridge from being a child to becoming friends. And understand that they are human, not just your parents, and that as much as they annoy you, you're probably annoying them too. It's just like roommates!"

More Ways to Conquer

I'm not one to put much stock in statistics. When I hear NFL commentators say things like, "This team has won the matchup six out of the last ten meetings over the past five years when the hot dog guys were wearing red," it makes me want to bang my head against the wall. But in this case, the statistics are telling and reassuring. According to the 2002 U.S. Census Bureau, 56.8 percent of men and

43.2 percent of women aged 22 to 31 live with their parents, and 56 percent of college students plan to move back in with their parents after graduation. You don't need me to interpret those statistics, but let me reiterate: more than half of college graduates live at their parents' homes. While in prior decades there might have been a stigma associated with moving back in with your parents, there shouldn't be anymore. It's become the norm.

If you feel embarrassed about living with your parents, it's probably because you believe that living with the 'rents reflects a failure or immaturity on your part, that you couldn't handle life alone, so Mom and/or Dad had to step in as they've done all your life. But especially if you have recently graduated, perhaps you should consider that your attitude and maturity now aren't much different from what they were a few years ago, or even last year. What, now that you've finished school, you're suddenly prepared to be an adult? Turn the tassle and, boom, immediately you can shed your childhood insecurities and needs and take on all adult responsibilities without help or support from anyone else? Not so much.

Moving in with the parents doesn't mean you have failed at anything. Actually, if you're able to do so, you should consider yourself lucky. Whether you live rent free or contribute to the household, such close proximity to the people who nurtured you through the first twentysomething years of your life means that your support network is right in front of you. You don't have to feel like you're muddling through your 20s alone if you're living with people who care about your well-being. The caveat is that while it's normal to temporarily depend on your parents as a safety net, it's not fair to them or to you to use them as a crutch. If you use a rent-free life as an excuse to loaf rather than sincerely trying to figure out how to support yourself, then you're not helping anyone. You want your parents to be assured that they're helping you learn to stand on your own, not delaying your self-sufficiency.

Part 5

Identity

By the time we graduate from school, whether it's high school or college, our external identity may be associated with our hobbies, family, background, or academic aptitude. We don't think we have an *adult* identity yet, one that has been both formed and informed by experiences and choices that we have made independently. But claiming that you can't move forward in life until you're older is a cop-out. Adulthood might refine your identity—your personality, your loves, your peeves, your motivations—but will not change who you are at your core. As cliché as it sounds, everything you're seeking can be found somewhere in the person you already are. You simply have to muster up the courage to go find it.

At the root of all the questions addressed in this book is the issue of identity. You cannot know what you want, or gauge how much you want it, until you have a solid sense of who you are. Perhaps a workable analogy is to compare it to giving gifts to someone. It's considerably easier to choose a good present for a friend you know well than for a stranger. The more thought and care you put into finding a suitable, personally tailored present, the more appreciated and rewarding the gift will be. Likewise, the life you choose for yourself will fit you better the more you know your personal tastes.

As you'll see in the mentors' answers in this chapter, what conquering your Quarterlife Crisis comes down to is knowing and accepting yourself. Even if you can successfully work through the advice for all of the previous questions in this book, you can't truly apply it until you understand the person you're applying it to. At some point in your life, you are going to have to face yourself and confront your identity—stripped down, vulnerable, and shed of protective layers like material goods, advanced degrees, and the pressures and expectations that you've internalized. You are Alice, leaping through the looking glass. You are Luke Skywalker, at Yoda's prodding, confronting your inner demons. It is the people who don't do this or put it off who either don't find happiness or eventually fall into a midlife crisis until they figure out the identity they've been muffling throughout their adulthood. We are the first generation to have the time, passion, and drive to face these tough issues in early adulthood rather than waiting until we're firmly ensconced in a life we don't want. We may be the first generation not to do better financially than our parents, but we do have the power to create happier lives at a younger age—an infinitely better advantage. At some point in your life, you are going to have to confront yourself. You might as well do it now.

Chapter 21

Why can't I deal with adulthood?

Julie Czerniewski, a 25-year-old from Michigan, started asking this adulthood question on New Year's Eve in 2003. New Year's Eve was always her biggest party night of the year; usually she attended large parties or traveled to exotic places. "So, imagine my surprise when this New Year's, while partying at a friend's house, all I wanted was to watch Dick Clark in the privacy of my own home. 'What on earth is happening to me?' I thought to myself as I watched everyone else drink up a storm and enjoy the night's festivities, as I usually did. 'Why am I sitting here, arms crossed, water in hand, counting down the minutes until I can go home and crawl into bed?' As I forced myself to at least stay through the ball drop, it hit me like a ton of bricks. I'm getting old," Julie says. "All of a sudden, a deep sadness came over me that lasted for several days. It can't be over: all the fun times I had through college and the few years since, can they possibly be over? Will my weekends now revolve around picking paint colors instead of bars? I know things change and we all grow up, but I'm just not ready for it. How can I bring myself to accept and maybe even prefer my new adult life?"

Laugh It into Perspective

MENTOR: Jill Neighbour

AGE: 27

I WISH I'D KNOWN AT 25 THAT "you shouldn't expect to follow a certain recipe just because you're a certain age."

Jill Neighbour, who graduated from Edinboro University of Pennsylvania in 1998, doesn't necessarily believe she has become a "real" adult. "I don't think I'm ready for that label, and don't know if I ever will be. But maybe that's how I deal with adulthood: I stay right on the outskirts. I firmly believe that age is just a number; it's how you feel. I don't feel 27; I don't think (fingers crossed) I'll feel 40 when I'm 40. I usually laugh at name analysis, but my name, Jill, means youthfulness. Yippee!" she says.

In recent years Jill has faced some pointed indications that she is growing older. "Lately I've had some of those little upper-cuts that remind you that you're no longer 18. For instance, I spent a year teaching in North Carolina. In my coed ninth grade health class, I was trying to explain type A personalities. The first person that popped into my head was Alex P. Keaton from *Family Ties*. I threw this out to the class and got nothing but blank stares. I tried it again: 'You know, Alex P. Keaton, Michael J. Fox, the guy from *Back to the Future* and *Teen Wolf* . . .' and again, got nothing. Now they had that wrinkled-up forehead look as though I were speaking a foreign language. Thanks guys. Then I tried, 'How about Monica Geller from *Friends*?' And the light came on!" Jill says. "Another kick in the pants came when I was on a long car trip. I was listening to what sounded like a country radio station. One great song played, great. The next one came on: again, great song, knew every word. A third great one in a row, singing along. Then the ad came on: 'Thank you for listening to blah blah blah *classic rock*.' The songs I remembered and loved, the ones they played at junior high (before it was called middle school), were now considered *classic rock!* Ouch!"

Jill says the only way she has learned that she can respond to these sorts of reminders, and to the onset of adulthood in general, is to laugh them off and take them in stride. "There are certain things in life you can't do anything about, and getting older is one of them. There's no point in getting all worked up and stressed out about the things we can't control. You've got two choices: get upset and frustrated with the changes in your body (gray hair, argh!) or with added responsibilities (insurance bills, car payments), or you can take everything with a grain of salt and laugh it off. I think the latter is the only healthy way to go about it," she says. "Another thing I like to keep in mind to put things in perspective is that no matter what, things could always be worse. For instance, I have gray hair, but at least I'm not losing my hair. Insurance bills are outrageous, but at least I can afford quality insurance. Also, I've surrounded myself with people who have similar philosophies on life and adulthood. This has really helped."

You're Not Alone

MENTOR: Julia Mallor

AGE: 23

I WISH I'D KNOWN AT 21 THAT "life is a marathon, not a sprint."

"Adulthood was not something I had the privilege of easing into. It was more or less thrown in my lap," says Julia Mallor, who married her college sweetheart in Salt Lake City just before her 22nd birthday. "Our future together held excitement and high hopes. But after being married for only two months and three weeks, our plans came to a screeching halt. I was at our apartment waiting for him when I received a phone call from a hospital chaplain. He informed me that my husband was in a car accident and I needed to come to the hospital right away. There was no explanation of the injuries he suffered or if he would suffer no more. I frantically gathered my purse and a roll of toilet paper for my tears and rushed to the emergency room. During times of trauma, things seem to move in slow motion. When the nurses brought me back to meet him, I held tight to the advice my mom gave me on the phone just before I left for the hospital. She told me that no matter what shape my husband was in, I had to be strong for him. When I saw him, I found out he was rear-ended on his way home by a semi. He suffered a traumatic brain injury and was in a coma. My whole world changed. I went from an innocent, naïve 22-year-old to a caregiver of a comatose person within about an hour."

Julia's husband remained in a coma for a month. "I would spend all day at the hospital afraid that if I left I would miss a medical miracle or, worse, that I would miss any turns for the worse. Throughout the day I got updates from the neurosurgeon, who seemed to speak a foreign language. During those critical times, I learned how to handle people in higher positions. I learned to become organized with my questions, to seek out any and all answers," she says. "On one update the doctor would be optimistic about his progress, and on another update her spirits wouldn't be as promising. Doctors would continually remind my family and me that this is a marathon and that we shouldn't run ourselves too quickly in the beginning because we will need to finish strong. Several fears went through my head with each update. The most prevalent at the time were, 'When is he going to wake up?' and 'Once he is awake, will he remember me, will he still know he is married, and worse, will he still love me?' The reality was that no one knew exactly when he was going to wake up and no one knew what he would be like. That's when I had to remind myself to put my faith into something I knew would hold firm no matter what the outcome. For me, that was my faith in God."

When Julia's husband awoke from the coma, it was the beginning of a tortuously long process. "He did not, as many movies portray, wake up and walk out of bed kissing and hugging all of us as if he had just awakened from a refreshing night's sleep. He opened his eyes, which had a glossed-over, dazed look, as if he wasn't looking at anything specific. The accident took a horrible toll on his physical status. It took three weeks to wean him off the ventilator. In the process, the nurses and therapist began to teach him how to live again. He couldn't sit up on his own without falling, he couldn't hold his head up for more than about five seconds, and, needless to say, he couldn't walk. This recovery process took us to several different hospitals, each specializing in a specific area," Julia says. "Within a relatively short period of time, he was able to come home to the home we had only spent a short time in as a married couple. I became his caregiver, waking up in the middle of the night to walk him to the bathroom, walking him downstairs to where a van would take him to therapy, and trying to maintain a strong attitude to keep us both encouraged. I remember the first time he walked unassisted. I was sitting on the couch when he walked about five steps. I called both of our moms. It was a great moment."

At the time of this writing, Julia's husband is walking, though with an awkward gait, and speaks with a slight mumble. He still goes to therapy four times a week to work on his speech and motor skills. Nobody knows how much better he'll get. "Although life as I know it will never be as simple as before, things continue to improve. Life keeps going whether we are ready for it or not. So how did I deal with this rush of adulthood? I held on to my faith. There were some points when I felt I was at my breaking point, but God would put someone in my path to lift me up. I had a great support network of family, friends, and church members. It's important to remember during difficult times to allow your friends and family to assist you. It takes a humble person to accept help from others," Julia says. "My experience as an adult is nothing like what I imagined it would be, but I'm not deprived by any means. I have a good job, good clothes, food, and shelter. I have a husband who loves me, but still, I thought it would be easier. I had a portrait in my head as to how adulthood would be. When I was a child, I thought adulthood meant freedom, travel, and independence. I'm now learning that this portrait is more of a fairy tale than reality. Not that adulthood is a nightmare; there's just more that goes into it than what you know and expect as a child."

Julia says that her experience taught her some valuable points about adulthood that could help other twentysomethings whether or not they face a similarly tragic situation. "Most readers will not have experienced a situation such as mine, but no matter what life event is causing someone stress, it's a big deal. It's important to free yourself of the preconceived ideas of what adulthood should be. The preconceived ideas are often what lead people into a downfall of hopes. God gives everyone a different deck of cards to play out; you should use what you have been given, good or bad, to the fullest," she says. "Also, recognize the importance of sharing your triumphs and struggles with others. Personally, I joined a Bible study, which allows me to free some of the bottled emotions I contain inside with people who share similar emotions or offer encouragement. It lets me know that no one is alone in this world if we reach out to others. Sharing my emotions with friends and remaining strong in my faith have been the staples that have kept me together."

Create Your Own Definition

MENTOR: Jake Dixon
AGE: 37
I WISH I'D KNOWN AT 25 THAT "adulthood is about character."

When Jake Dixon was in his early 20s, he skipped college to play in several bands, "living the bohemian life to the hilt." After quitting the drugs and alcohol associated with the lifestyle he was leading, Jake intensely questioned what adulthood meant and how close he was to that stage. "My parents were solid products of the 1940s and 1950s: You're supposed to attend college, get married, get a career and mortgage, raise children, no questions asked. Duty and responsibility? Grit your teeth and bear it. That was what adulthood was all about," he says. "Then, as I grew up, divorce rates skyrocketed and capitalism went global. Careers became serialized, the temp sector increased dramatically, and technology changed the structure of business. It became okay to forgo children to concentrate on careers because those careers could no longer be taken for granted. The things I was raised to believe as the vehicles to maturity seemed untenable. My questions kept coming. In the '90s and '00s, a legal pharmaceutically engineered life became a real possibility. With the onslaught of new wonder drugs, it's hard to know what it means to handle the stresses of life as an adult (if I take Prozac, have I thrown in the towel in some sense?)."

When Jake sought therapy to deal with his confusion, the doctor diagnosed him as depressed and offered him a Prozac prescription. Jake didn't take it. "It wasn't a misdiagnosis, but there were better ways to deal with this: exercise, eating better, regular sleep, for instance. Compounding this depression was the endless profusion of career choices confronting me," he says. "I was forced to conclude that, in our smorgasbord of freedoms and possible identities, 'adulthood' somehow became a lifestyle choice. Many people my age had married, had serial careers, and had bought all the accoutrements of a placid bourgeois life, I observed, yet in their social lives and in the manner in which they interacted with people, they seemed to be still playing tired old high school games, but now with power, prestige, Beemers, and caterers. They complained about something missing from the picture, having discovered a void within; they were searching even after finding marriage, children, and measures of applause. What is adulthood, anyway?"

Jake eventually came to terms with adulthood by redefining the term for himself rather than adhering to society's standards of what an "adult" should be. "For me, spirituality gave the answers. I remember the vertigo of my early and mid-20s, the restlessness and paralysis caused by the sense of limitless possibilities before me. I studied many traditions but kept coming back to Buddhism with its emphasis on impermanence and our self-created suffering. By my early 30s, my answer to the question had become that it was about *character* and that character was created in how we dealt with impermanence. One's character is truly shown in dealing with the random monkey wrenches thrown into our plans and how one accepts finitude of life, career, and relationships. Adulthood, then, consists in knowing that I'm not the one really in control of events, but I am in control of my reaction to them. I decided I would do my best, but the outcome was out of my hands. It's simple. And I've become much happier."

More Ways to Conquer

One of the major identity quandaries of the Quarterlife Crisis is that because of our age, people want to see us as adults even if we may not be ready to be viewed that way. When we emerge from school, we're immediately expected to make a slew of decisions that we aren't equipped to make. As we choose career paths, places to live, people to date, and lifestyles to follow—things for which we have had little to no real-world training—it can feel like we're pretending to be adults, just going through the motions. It can feel like we're playing house.

As we march inevitably and reluctantly toward Age and Adulthood, one of the scariest feelings can be the sense that we must let go of our childhood. Whether our childhood was idyllic or we merely associate it with fewer worries and a less jaded outlook, many of us fear leaving it behind and instead struggle to remain in or strive to recapture the joy and security of those simpler times. Sometimes circumstances force us to face unexpected responsibilities.

But there are other options. Jake hit upon a solution that works for many twentysomethings: if you're not happy with the way adulthood is defined, then redefine it for yourself. Whether you focus on character growth or spirituality, tangible landmarks or personal revelations, you can turn your journey to and through adulthood into the path you want it to be. First you might figure out what it means to you to be an adult, or what characterizes the adult you want to be. Then you gradually shed the things you've outgrown but allow yourself to cling to the parts of your past that you'd like to take with you. While we form our personal frameworks of adulthood, we're lucky that we happen to be making this transition during a time when there is a larger movement toward redefining this phase. The Introduction touched on this new way of looking at the 20s and the way that traditional landmarks such as marriage and careers have shifted so that "30 is the new 20." We can take some solace in that certain sectors of society are willing to change their perceptions as we have changed with the times.

Another way to look at this question is that this is an issue that comes down to comparisons and expectations. You have no obligation to live through stages of life that were constructed by other people. You can live your life on your terms without care to how other people are living theirs. Simply because society brands you with a label doesn't mean you have to accept it. It may be easiest to ignore labels like adulthood and go with the flow of your life without regard to the names people give certain phases. Inner growth is completely subjective and perhaps progresses best when unconstrained.

Chapter 22

What do I do if my life seems boring or meaningless?

Jim Wood, a 24-year-old in Georgia, thought life was going terrifically until his job as a police officer was tainted by politics, his wife cheated on him, and he filed for divorce. Now single and working at a corporate security firm, Jim gets depressed because of what he feels is a lack of meaning in his life. "I've got my job, but outside of that there's nothing else. After work I go home. I'm tired of the routine and I need a change, but I really don't know what that change should be. I'm trying to fill the void left by my relationship. I had someone to spend time with, confide in, do things with. Now that that's gone, I feel like I'm going crazy. I have nothing to occupy my time," he says. "My parents got married young and have been together ever since. I was brought up in a household where I felt like, you get married, that's it. Now I'm here and that's what I want: to be settled down, married, have kids, a normal job with normal hours. To me, that's what gives life meaning, what makes it all worthwhile. I'm extremely bored when I'm not at work. I feel like there is not any meaning in my life. I feel like I'm spinning out of control."

For some twentysomethings, this question applies even if we know the situation is only temporary. Kira Dickson, 26, is currently in this kind of holding pattern. "I am definitely in a bit of a life co-nundrum right now. I've been working in the same job, as an assistant director of communication at a private girls school, for three years. It's an interesting job most of the time, and I'm able to coach soccer. However, my job has some really dead times, and I'm not the head of my department. I work mainly with women who are older than me by at least fifteen years," Kira says. "Then there's the contrast with my life outside of work. I'm newly married to a wonderful man who recently began a new career and is enjoying every new day. Here's my conundrum: What do I do with myself between now and when we have kids? I'd definitely be interested in looking into a new field, but then how long would I be there? My husband and I are lucky enough to be financially stable, which means I'll be able to stay home when we start having kids. This is what I've been planning to do as long as I've been planning. There's no job I'd rather have than stay-at-home mom." But why? I often wonder why I exist now. Why did I spend so many years at an Ivy League school and getting my master's degree? What *do* I do if my life seems boring and meaningless?"

Don't Feel Guilty about Focusing on You

MENTOR: Shadiin D. Garcia

AGE: 29

I WISH I'D KNOWN AT 27 THAT "it's easy to hate yourself if you buy the myth that only one thing should fulfill you."

When Oregon resident Shadiin Garcia was 25, she and her husband, then a graduate student, knew they wanted to have children but weren't sure when the time would be right. One of her husband's professors gave him the advice, "There will never be a convenient time to have kids. If you want them, just have them." Believing the advice was sound, Shadiin and her husband went ahead with it. "In hindsight, we probably had our first son at the most inconvenient time possible. I was a full-time teacher in an inner city school, raising my 16-year-old brother, and volunteering fifteen hours a week for an after-school program while my husband was at home writing his dissertation. To help make ends meet, I also worked as the official scorekeeper at local basketball games and as a proctor for standardized tests. When I had Gabriel, I wasn't even sort of prepared for motherhood," Shadiin says.

Soon after she had her son, Shadiin found herself in a situation she had never expected: she was extremely bored and frustrated. "The hardest thing for me wasn't changing diapers or dealing with a crying baby; it was having the rest of my life come to a sudden halt. Before I had Gabriel, my day usually started at 6:30 a.m., when I would meet students in my classroom for extra tutoring, then teach a full day, run the after-school tutoring program, and then the day would end around 9:30 at night, depending on what time the basketball game let out. If there wasn't a game, I was usually at the kitchen table helping my brother with his homework. To go from working out of the house constantly to being at home with a newborn was shocking. I had thought it would be fantastic and that I would be totally fulfilled being a mom. But the reality of it was that I was bored to tears. I was so angry with myself and embarrassed that motherhood wasn't fulfilling me, but I never wanted to let on that I was miserable. I love my son more than anything, but I wasn't prepared to hate myself in the process. It's like an unspoken thing, too. Once I mentioned it to other people, only a few would willingly admit that they too were bored and had a hard time realizing that life as they knew it was over. While my husband was living his dream life of writing, researching, and playing with great colleagues, I was at home cleaning, changing diapers, tutoring my brother, and crawling with Gabe. I couldn't believe this was my life. What happened to the woman I was supposed to become? All of my other friends were doing things like speaking at conferences in Geneva and working for human rights in South America, and here I was at home with the most beautiful boy, but still at home."

Shadiin's first step was to address what she realized was a mild case of postpartum depression. Once she noticed that she would start crying every day at noon, she did things to prevent it. She found that if at 11 a.m. she went for a ten-minute walk, then she wouldn't feel sad. The routine "worked like a charm" to ease the depression, but she still couldn't handle her feelings of boredom. A few months later, Shadiin and her family moved to a new city, and her brother, who ended his school year with better grades, moved back in with his father.

Still not entirely fulfilled, Shadiin decided to go back to work as a tutor, working from 3:30 to 8 p.m. four days a week while her husband watched their son at home. She also hired a babysitter to come in for three hours a day, three mornings a week. And she took in her cousin as a foster child to help her graduate from high school. "We couldn't even afford the babysitter, but neither could we afford my spiraling into despair. The arrangement was fantastic. There was so much going on once I started work that life was good again," Shadiin says. "I never in a million years would have thought this was where my life would be, but I was so happy to finally be in a position where I could help my family. I am Chicana and Laguna Pueblo from New Mexico, my mother is one of nine and my father is one of seven, and I have more than forty first cousins. Very few of my cousins have made it this far in terms of schooling, and I feel so lucky to be able to help out my family now. When I left home at 16 for a better school and ultimately a better life, I felt so guilty about those I left behind. But now I'm fulfilling my dream of being able to help my cousins and my brother realize their dreams as well."

People constantly ask Shadiin how she was able to begin to raise her children, take in foster children, and subsist on her and her husband's small salaries. The truth is, she says, they "really didn't manage it." They went into debt. "But now that my husband is a professor, we are slowly chipping away at the debt, and I think it was worth it. I have two sons now, but no more teens. Because my second son almost died when he was born, I have a different outlook on motherhood. I also know my limits, so I'm working part time to stay sane, taking one class in grad school, and watching my sons grow the rest of the time," Shadiin says. "I learned that meaning can only be achieved in life if you are helping others. And if we do indeed decide that our life is boring and meaningless, then we have to look again at what we used to feel passionate about and find a balance. And most important, I've learned that it is entirely possible and perhaps expected to feel isolation and happiness at the same time, to feel anger and love at the same time, to feel cheated and fulfilled at the same time. I had no idea that these emotions could be held side by side and that I did *not* have to feel guilty about it."

Challenge Yourself

MENTOR: Captain Alexander Snowden

AGE: 32

I WISH I'D KNOWN AT 21 THAT "as you look back, you'll want to say you had a lot of experiences. You don't want to take for granted your youth, vigor, and energy."

When Memphis, Tennessee native Alexander Snowden graduated from college, he and a friend hit the road, ready to conquer the world. "I can still remember the absolute feeling of jubilation of hitting the 'real world' and no longer being considered a student. We packed our clothes and all of our belongings into a rental van and zoomed to Denver," Alexander says. "Within months, every thought of joining a marketing company and hopping on the fast track to success had turned into an illusion. Why did I think this was going to be so easy? All of a sudden, I felt like a freshman again. But this time, I wasn't in college. I was a freshman in life. My roommate immediately got his residential realtor's license. I, on the other hand, naïvely joined a sales company similar to Amway that left me broke and in disbelief. The shock and horror of realizing the world didn't owe me a thing and wasn't going to welcome me with open arms after graduation hit me like a ton of bricks."

Out of money, Alexander moved back to his parents' place in Memphis, where he had a strong support group of family and friends. In response to his father's continuous badgering with the question, "Now what're you going to do?" Alexander began working for a company that sold copiers and mailer devices, figuring he had to get some sales experience before he could get hired in a better sales position. "I went into it head first. Then, one day I strolled past a colleague who was twenty-some-odd years older than I was. I asked him how long he had been there. His reply astonished me. He said he had been there for almost fifteen years. I couldn't believe it. For fifteen years, day in and day out, he sat behind a cubicle. I turned 25 and realized I was very unhappy. Was this it? Was this what all my energy and youth was going towards? I didn't want to stop living. I didn't want to sit behind a cubicle. I wanted to be a student again. At least in school I had goals and worked towards an end. Now, I felt like I worked just to make ends meet, and there wasn't an end. I was scared," Alexander says.

One day, in between sales calls, Alexander happened to pass by a military recruiting station. "I don't know why I walked in, but I did. I had something to offer. I didn't want to have to answer a young kid's question with, 'I've been sitting behind this desk for fifteen years.' I had an hour to kill before my next sales call. I opened the door and nervously went in. I went to each of the branches of service besides the Air Force and asked questions. The Navy didn't want me because I didn't have an engineer's degree. The Army kept calling me a general to hype me up. And then I walked into the Marines' office. They didn't care who I was. They didn't jump up. I almost left, but then I thought if I were going to do something that I could always look back on and be proud of for the rest of my life, then the Marines would definitely give it to me. I was young, dammit. I had something to offer in life. No one else seemed to see this, or care, in the work world. I wanted to challenge myself, and sitting behind a desk wasn't the challenge I sought," Alexander says.

"I never, ever imagined joining the military. While in a fraternity in college, I scoffed at the ROTC candidates as they marched by while I cracked open a beer as my salute. I would've never made it if I had joined ROTC in college. The timing wasn't right. After two frustrating years in the real world after college, the timing was right that day. After a year and a half of intense training and many sleepless nights in infantry officer school, I found myself leading a platoon (approximately forty-three) of Marines in combat in war-torn Kosovo."

Since then, Alexander has risen in the Marine Corps ranks to captain and says his life has changed completely. He says, "In my late 20s I was doing something that had more meaning than anything I could ever imagine. I felt as though I had climbed Mount Everest and lived to tell about it. Now I see the world in a whole new light. My respect for people in general has blossomed tremendously. Now that I'm 32 and have challenged myself, my priorities are changing. I plan to get out of the Marine Corps in a year and back to a sales position. Why? Things are different now. The back is a little sore, and my knees remind me daily that I can't run with a pack on my back as well as I used to just seven years ago when I strolled into the recruiters' office. I feel more fulfilled, and I'm satisfied with the challenges that I've met both physically and mentally. Therefore, I want to challenge myself in other ways now, with a home, a dog, and a wife and kids. I am positive that life will equal the Marine Corps in mental and physical prowess. By the time I get out of the Marine Corps, I will be 33 years old and ready to start afresh. Who knows? You might find me coming by your office with something under my arm to sell. But you know what? I'll have a huge smile on my face because I've got nothing left to prove to myself."

Alexander's tips for twentysomethings who feel like their lives are boring and meaningless include the following:

Challenge yourself. "The young years of life in your 20s and 30s are wonderful. It's a time to challenge yourself, take risks, and do things you'll be proud to look back on. I didn't want to be the guy who takes up hang gliding at age 45 because he felt like he hadn't done anything in life. I want to be the guy who looks back and thinks he did everything he could in his youth while he still had the energy and vitality."

Choose energizing goals. "It's not just about the military. For someone else it could be a passion for building, speaking publicly, or running for office. Whatever it is, our minds and bodies are driven to work toward that goal. When we're children, we have dreams to fly, write, be a chef, and so on. When we don't listen to ourselves, we end up looking back after twenty years and asking ourselves if we were really happy in life."

Don't prioritize money. "Don't worry about the money. I didn't join the Marines for money. Do the things you love. If people see your passion in life, they will want you to lead, you'll be promoted, and the money will eventually come."

Take the Initiative to Join

MENTOR: Kristen Pasculli
AGE: 25
I WISH I'D KNOWN AT 21 THAT "I'd really have to seek out what I wanted. Things don't just come to you."

When Kristen Pasculli attended Stockton College, "meaning was everywhere" because everything she did had a clear goal. "Go to class; get a degree. Volunteer; brighten hearts and meet awesome people. Hang out with friends; make lifelong friendships. Once out of college, social circles dwindled and so did my abilities to help others. Now that the opportunities to do good things are harder to come by, I have to seek them out. I had to get back out there and get involved," Kristen says. "So I now read newspapers to find groups to join and events to attend. It takes work, but if I sat inside and moped, life would be meaningless. I think as long as

I keep trying to get involved through social and service activities, my life has meaning. And it's okay to feel alone and worthless, but I can't let negative self-talk take over. So unless I seek out ways to give my life meaning, it really won't have it. That's the thing—even though life is now 9 a.m. to 5 p.m. nonstop, I have to make time to read, write, paint, and volunteer. These things aren't just hobbies: they help me contribute to the world and keep learning about myself. As long as I'm doing those things, my life has greater meaning. 'Cause let's face it, just working will send you into depression. Twentysomethings just have to be aware that they can still feel empowered, but after college they have to take more initiative."

More Ways to Conquer

The mentors in this section have some insightful ideas as to how to combat what seems like a boring and meaningless existence. After having discussed this issue with scores of other twentysomethings, I can add four more possible ways to jump-start your life, to inject meaning and excitement.

Get Outside Your Comfort Zone

When we settle into a life of monotony, when the days blur into one another, those are signs that we're not challenging ourselves; rather than pushing ourselves to explore and broaden, we're stuck in a rut of unsatisfactory sameness. To leap out of this rut, many twentysomethings have had success by challenging their sense of comfort. I have a friend who every year on her birthday forces herself to do something she calls "outside of my comfort zone." One year it was skydiving. Another year it was traveling to another country. By continuously expanding her boundaries, she is constantly learning about the world and about herself. By exposing your mind to possibilities you previously considered beyond your limits, chances are you'll find a ladder to grab onto that will lift you out of your funk.

Find a Connection

Whether spiritual, emotional, or inspirational, a connection with someone or something most likely will make you feel better about your life. This could be something as involved as religion or as casual as volunteering for a community service event. To find an emotional connection doesn't mean to go out and get a date; if you have room for the commitment, even a pet can change your life. Finding a connection can also be as simple as learning to be in tune with things you like and then doing those things repeatedly, like listening to a specific type of music, undertaking some sort of craft or carpentry, or visiting someone you love.

Make Your Own Luck

This tip comes courtesy of Brad Kennedy, a mentor in the last chapter in this book. He says, "One concept I like is doing more than one thing to get from one place to another. For example, people are very tied, creatures of habit that they are, to the idea of doing one job. But if you look at many people who have been successful in terms of working and building security, they did all kinds of jobs that existed on parallel tracks. Those same people often continue that practice even after they become what someone else might call successful. This is a form of not having your eggs all in one basket. Likewise, in finding romantic relationships, people fall into self-limiting patterns. They go to the same bar with the same friends, or they feel lazy about the whole process and try online dating, doing virtually nothing else. If I select fifty-one cards to hold in my hand, I am much more likely to have four aces than if I select four cards. No probability theory at all is needed to understand that, but most people don't apply the concept."

Don't Be Afraid to Buck Convention

Perhaps you feel your life is boring and meaningless because the lifestyle you're leading is one of convention rather than one you desire. There is no mandate that your life must consist of certain things: a desk job, a regular salary, an apartment in the city, one romantic partner. If particular aspects of your life aren't working for you, change them. Create your own tracks. The more you learn about various alternatives, the more likely you'll be to happen upon something that works for you.

Chapter 23

How do I stop feeling so overwhelmed?

For Mary Nersessian, 22, the overwhelming feelings began in her last year at Ryerson University in Toronto. Along with her fears of impending adulthood, Mary was juggling tough assignments, trying to find a job, applying to grad school, working insane hours at a local newspaper, and volunteering in her community. "I thought I was going crazy. Finding a job in journalism is notoriously competitive, and although I had some experience, I compared myself to people who had more than I did. I felt like I couldn't catch up, and I didn't know what I wanted to do. I applied to grad school programs I wasn't even sure I wanted to take," Mary says. "I called what I and most students I knew were going through the 'grad plague,' a feeling of discontent and being overwhelmed, unsure about how to take the first step into the rest of our lives. This was in addition to sleepless nights and growing resentment at the people who constantly asked us what we would be doing when we graduated, and the unclear idea of why we entered the program four years ago."

Accept the Chaos

MENTOR: Raquel Aviva

AGE: 32

I WISH I'D KNOWN AT 27 THAT "sometimes your life has to take a different path to take you where you need to be."

The year Raquel Aviva was 27 was the worst year of her life. Her grandmother, Raquel's "everything," died, as did four other relatives; her parents divorced after thirty-two years of marriage; her dog was in an accident; Raquel and her boyfriend broke up and he moved out; and after ten years working for Nickelodeon, where she had started as an intern and worked her way up to employee of the year, she had to leave her job. "I call it the year of shaking up the snow globe. There was no foundation left. Everything from my past existence disappeared. Everything I was used to leaning on suddenly wasn't there anymore," she says. "I was in so much pain. The changes I was going through made it a really hurtful time, and I had dark moments. The whole year was turmoil."

At first, Raquel allowed herself to be upset. After she went through the natural sad and angry stages of mourning, for her grandmother and for her life, she tried dealing with the situation by escaping it. "Usually I'm pretty strong, but every aspect of my life had changed. I turned around and there was a completely different landscape, so I focused my energy on getting out of town," she says. "I created distractions, which was good. I needed that at the moment. Some people work out like fiends. I kissed a couple boys, but I never went over the top."

Eventually, Raquel realized that to get through this tumultuous part of her life, she was going to have to "plow through it." After trying on her own to face her new life head-on, she turned to therapy for help. "I'm a fighter. Usually I can get through things, but I decided I needed an outside person to talk to because this time it was all too heavy. I asked a couple friends to recommend therapists, and I found a great one. It helped to talk it out," she says. "I was an anxious person. (I'm an Italian Jew. Anxiety is just there.) Therapy helped me reteach myself how to deal with stress in a normal way. I learned not to be so anxious. What will be, will be."

One way she learned to cope was by finding ways to "release." Although she disliked exercising, Raquel began taking yoga classes, which she loved immediately. "Some people go to a gym or roller skate. Yoga totally helped me to become centered. When you're overwhelmed, you need to find your thing that makes you release and get yourself centered again. For me, that was yoga, dancing, and even karaoke."

Rather than dwell on her losses, Raquel made sure she occupied her mind with other thoughts. "I didn't let myself think too much about it. When I caught myself thinking negative thoughts, I brought myself back to a positive space by not allowing them to get in my head. I just said, 'Stop.' When I had to, I had a group of songs I put on when I knew I needed a good cry. Then I let it happen, but I didn't let it pull me down into the whirlwind that I used to. I didn't let it ruin my day. I would say, 'Okay, that's a sad moment, and I know it's there, but now I'm going to move on to the next thing.' "

Slowly, Raquel put the pieces of her life together in a different way. When she left Nickelodeon, her boss told her to do something relating to music, her first love. After freelancing, she snagged a job at MTV that she still loves. When she was 29, she met a new guy whom she has been with ever since. And now, at 32, Raquel believes that the pandemonium in her life was a necessary chaos. "I kept saying, 'What is the lesson? What am I supposed to be learning?' It does get better. I had to learn about empowering myself to embrace changes and see how it could work," she says. "Looking back, I'm so glad I had to uproot everything, but going through the process was so difficult. I needed to be here because I wasn't doing what I was supposed to be doing before. I had to readjust the road I was on. I had to back up to the fork and take another direction."

Prioritize to *Your* Preferences

MENTOR: Jacob Rolls

AGE: 26

I WISH I'D KNOWN AT 25 THAT "it's okay to say no."

Last year, Jacob Rolls, a 2000 graduate of Texas State University, spent an average of nineteen hours a day at law school, where he worked in a clinical program, served as a teacher's assistant, edited assignments for the law review, and did his own classwork. "I checked my voice mails around once a week, and I missed bill payments, birthdays, appointments, and sunshine. At one point, after a string of successive all-nighters, I broke down crying. I think that was the first time I was completely physically, mentally, and spiritually exhausted. In trying to make myself feel *productive,* I had pushed it too far," Jacob says. "It wasn't until I was overwhelmed that I realized I'd have to adopt a workable strategy to balance my personal interests with my capabilities."

Once Jacob realized that he didn't have to stretch himself so far, he developed a new strategy for choosing which commitments to accept and prioritizing those responsibilities. "After discovering there are limits to what I can accomplish, and how miserable it is to exceed those limits, I decided to budget in 'me time' when making decisions about whether to take on new responsibilities. I've also found that friends and mentors who seem more balanced than me are great sources for advice concerning reasonable limits, and great listeners when I'm feeling particularly overwhelmed. I consider their advice, and I try to prioritize and evaluate current and potential obligations before accepting new responsibilities," he says.

"Once I'm able to make a somewhat informed decision about what I can handle, I tell the friends, family, colleagues, or supervisors who are expecting something from me. I've found they generally respect limits on my ability to take on increased responsibilities if I communicate those limitations in advance of deadlines or if I accept the responsibilities with reservations. Setting these boundaries gives me enough downtime to recover from the stress of a tight schedule. The single greatest piece of advice I can offer to people feeling overwhelmed who can't rework their schedule is to take a step back, take a deep breath, regroup, and talk to someone. This puts my stress into context and helps me come up with different ideas for dealing with it."

Focus on One Tangible Goal

MENTOR: Brady Muth

AGE: 26

I WISH I'D KNOWN AT 24 THAT "control only happens when you let go. Deal with things as they come to you rather than trying to control things before they happen."

When Brady Muth met his wife through mutual friends, he fell in love with her and with the son she was raising on her own. Less than a month after they were married, his wife became pregnant. Eight and a half months into the pregnancy, she had a brain aneurysm and died. Brady's world was shattered. On top of that, Brady, who had just begun his job as a teacher and athletic coach, was sued for custody of his son and his new daughter (who was delivered by cesarean section), a battle he eventually won. "I guess my kids are all I need to help me keep moving," Brady says. "Today Hannah is 1½ and a healthy, smart, beautiful baby. There is peace in finding some understanding of your place in the world and the crises you encounter. In dealing with my loss, I had to remember that it was just that: my loss. And the way I handled it was something I could control. I had a job to do and a life here yet to experience. What I've gone through sometimes doesn't seem real. If there's anyone else out there who lost a spouse so young, I would like them to know it happens and you can survive. It is possible."

One way Brady was able to get through this period was by focusing his energies on a specific, tangible goal and allowing other people to help put his feelings into perspective. "I bought a townhouse the summer after my wife passed. I gutted it and remodeled it, so that kept me busy. My kids helped me to focus on the positive things in life. My family and friends were great. My hometown of Yankton, South Dakota, has a population of about 15,000, and the whole community rallied around my family. I met a man who lost his wife in an accident, and he told me that he thought *he* had it bad. In his attempt to pat me on the back, we had a good laugh, and we both learned that life could always be worse. One has to realize the life you experience will always be the best possible path for you. I guess if this is as good or the best it gets, I wouldn't want to experience anything less," Brady says.

More Ways to Conquer

Maybe you feel overwhelmed because something tragic has happened in your life, as it did for Brady. Or maybe you feel overwhelmed because you're trying to balance all of the various uncertain aspects of life that we're somehow expected to come to terms with in our 20s. Either way, you've heard this before, but it bears repeating: accept what you can and cannot control. There will be events and circumstances in your life that you can't help, and at some point you must realize that stressing over them won't change them. As for things that you *can* control, the advice from the chapter on "What if I feel like I'm stuck?" is applicable here: take small steps. Anything that is overwhelming to you can be broken down into smaller, more manageable pieces.

Here are a few other ways to attack the various causes of your overwhelmed feelings:

Save Time by Trading

If you feel overwhelmed because it seems like you don't have enough time to deal with the various issues in your life, one time-saving idea is to trade skills with friends. Each of you offers to do something you're good at for the other, in exchange for the same. For example, if your Internet is down and you don't have time to deal with it, maybe a computer-savvy friend can take care of it (or deal with tech support), and in exchange you can edit the friend's résumé. Or you can dog-sit for another friend, who in return can do a round of grocery shopping for you. Exchanging little things for little things adds up to time saved, plus it's a way to lean on friends for support without feeling like you're freeloading.

Pare Down Options

One reason our generation experiences the Quarterlife Crisis more intensely than previous generations is because we have more options. It sounds backward that the more options we have, the more pressure we feel, but it's true. When we're expected to make decisions in our 20s, we're not usually choosing between two simple black-and-white options. We're choosing from among millions, whether the choice involves jobs, career paths, homes, friends, activities, or lifestyles. The vast array of opportunities, which have increased astronomically since our parents were in their 20s, doesn't always feel like the privilege it might be. It feels like chaos. So one way to make these choices seem less overwhelming is to limit your own options. The same way it's easier to choose from chicken or beef than to select an entree from a twenty-page menu, it's easier to make decisions and follow through with them when you can narrow down the list from which you allow yourself to choose.

Throw Yourself into Something You Love

Another way to work through overwhelming feelings is to throw yourself into something you care about, just as Brady fixed up a house and Raquel found her "release." Immersing yourself in something fulfilling allows you to forget about other things for a while. And when you're finished with the activity, your stress or pain is perhaps dulled a bit so that you can come at it with a clearer head and a fresher perspective, kind of like when you wake up in the morning after a good night's sleep.

Chapter 24

When will I stop feeling afraid of and start looking forward to growing older?

Heidi Padawer, a 24-year-old in St. Louis, says she can't comprehend how life could possibly get better with age. "I'm terrified of death. Dying. Being old. Being slow, feeble, incompetent. Limping when I walk, pursing my lips at loud noises ('kids in cars with their loud music'). To me, getting older isn't getting better or wiser or experienced; it's getting finicky, getting on society's nerves, becoming my own albatross. I tried to figure out what pains me so much about getting older. What am I losing, anyway, but a healthy dose of self-righteousness seasoned with a dollop of absolute ignorance? Maybe it's true what Cat Stevens said: 'You will still be here tomorrow, but your dreams may not,'" Heidi says.

"I guess the dream of my youth is the dream of glorified firsts: first love, first real job, first apartment, first Pottery Barn couch. So rather than be the person who relives her would-be glory days, I'd rather just not end the glory itself. As a result, I think getting old is like throwing in the towel on risk and adventure: old people get married, get pensions, get time-shares. Young people are a walking window on the world: my grandfather's eyes glisten when he tells his own stories, yet they light up when he retells mine. I know it's wrong to be this indulgent in my own life, but I can't help but be terrified that getting older will breed in me contempt for my own life, my pitfalls and personal shortcomings. As long as I'm young, I can do it all."

Hang On 'til 30

MENTOR: Trey Sampson
AGE: 34
I WISH I'D KNOWN AT 25 THAT "personal esteem and public image have only a tiny overlap."

"Quick answer," says Trey Sampson, "Age 30. When I turned 30, suddenly all the bullshit worries about why I hadn't earned a million dollars, written a novel, or made a film started to subside. Instead of comparing myself to the 28-year-old success stories in the *New York Times,* I started comparing myself to the people I really respected: writers and artists who didn't hit their stride until age 40, entrepreneurs who didn't find their true calling until age 50, etc. It's nice to be the young phenom, but the fate of a phenom is to disappear so that the rest of the world can say, 'Whatever happened to . . .?' Once you realize that the world is built for people who can deliver over the long haul, things calm down considerably."

Anticipate New Adventures

MENTOR: Lauren Randall
AGE: 25
I WISH I'D KNOWN AT 20 THAT "most people who are close to their families experience sadness in letting go of their childhood family life."

Lauren Randall remembers believing in the idea that youth was the best time of her life because she had trouble letting go of fond memories of high school and college. "It only becomes harder when I go back to college or my hometown of York, Pennsylvania, and realize it wasn't these places but the *people* that gave magic to those times. But even when I see many of these people,

I'm often sad because I know we've grown up and our friendships will never be the same. Times in high school and college seemed like the best because almost everything was about socializing and good times. But now, in graduate school, I spend most of my time focusing on my studies and only a few hours each week with friends. I realize this will only become more difficult when I work full time."

Lauren had difficulty looking forward to becoming older and wiser because she didn't want to let go of living at home and the close relationship she had with her family. "When I left for college, I wasn't seriously homesick, but I was sad that, as a fact of life, I had to get used to going from seeing my parents every day to every few weeks or months. It was almost like a grieving process, where I had to let go of all I had known. My parents helped by reminding me that I was exactly where I should have been at that point in my life," she says.

Lauren says it still isn't easy not being able to see her family on a daily basis as she gets older, but as she has come to accept that as a necessary part of growing up, she has been able to come to terms with it. "There's no way around these feelings of sadness, but you can't let them hold you back. It's a part of loving other people. I still call my parents almost every day and go home for holidays and many other random weekends. The best way for me to cope with these feelings is to be honest about them. I always miss them the most when I say goodbye after a visit. It's easiest to call them to tell them this and express how much I enjoyed our time together," she says.

Now Lauren is at a point in her life where she has found she is able to look forward to becoming older and wiser, rather than dwelling on the past. "When you go away to see a new part of the world, you'll discover things about yourself that you would never have known if you hadn't left your family; it's bittersweet but worthwhile. Every time I return home, now I'm reminded how much I have become my own person. My core values are the same as before I left home, but college and living in a different city has exposed me to new ideas. Since leaving home, I've changed political parties and religions. Who knows what new self-discoveries are to come?" she says. "I often feel like an 8-year-old masquerading as an adult, but I also feel like I've finally arrived, and it's a great feeling."

Your Confidence Will Skyrocket

MENTOR: Pam Hess
AGE: 36

I WISH I'D KNOWN AT 25 THAT "you'll care so little ten years later what any guy thinks of you at 25, and you'll save so much energy not worrying about it."

Pam Hess, an American University graduate who says this is her favorite question in this book, says that at 36, she has a number of thoughts on this issue. "First, we are the only species that keeps track of our age. Second, the alternative to getting older is dying, and as someone close to me died at age 24 on her daughter's second birthday, I can promise you that aging is far better," Pam says. "Except for a few body issues (I effortlessly weighed about eight pounds less ten years ago), I look better and feel better about myself now than I ever have. I also have much better fashion sense. What I've given up in metabolism and pink cheeks, I have more than made up for in confidence, willingness to take less shit from men, higher income (to pay for massages, excellent vacations, great dinners, my own house!)."

Pam says the most important benefit of aging is the confidence. When I think how much energy I spent in my 20s worrying about what some guy thought of me, or what some friend thought, or what strangers on the street thought, it exhausts me. Imagine what I would have accomplished if I had invested the energy I funneled into worrying about boys into my career, volunteer work, or traveling. One morning when I was 31, I woke up and went through my day and at the end of it realized not once did I ever wonder what anyone else thought of me, and neither did I care. A fantastic feeling of lightness. I don't think it's something you can consciously develop, though. I think that insecurity eventually exhausts itself, and then you find out in your 30s how *great* you are. And then you wonder what the hell you were so worried about before. Hang in there. It will happen if you let it."

More Ways to Conquer

As you get older, you get to know yourself better and doubt yourself less. Confidence grows with age, as you increase and diversify your experiences and broaden your awareness of different possibilities and alternatives. You learn about more options that you'll find rewarding and how to pursue those alternatives. You will add to the number of people you love; you will add to the number of things that make you happy.

Youth and adulthood aren't stages on either side of a line drawn at 25, 30, or 40. In fact, the people who believe that youth will have been the best time of their lives are often the people who associate "youth" with their childhood, the less complex time before you even thought to begin asking yourself the kinds of questions that are in this book. It is a falsehood that the best days of your life are behind you. Each and every thirtysomething with whom I discussed this question told me that their 30s have been better than their 20s. With age comes security, peace of mind, and peace with yourself. If you can't accept that now, know that you will eventually learn that the best times of your life are yet to come.

Chapter 25

What if I don't like myself? or,
Will I ever be happy?

Before Derek Manning, 24, graduated from college, his parents got divorced and his father moved to New England, hundreds of miles away from Derek's childhood home. Now Derek lives in a city in which he knows no one his age and hasn't yet found a job beyond menial service work. The combination of Derek's home life, job situation, and lack of social life causes him to "burst into spontaneous crying fits" out of frustration—fits that antidepressants and therapy haven't been able to lessen. "Oh, my God, I feel so horrible. I feel like I'm wasting away. I think to myself things like, 'Your dad paid 100 grand to send you to this fancy-ass college so you could get a job that doesn't even require a degree.' I feel like a loser," he says. "The real world is a lot harder than I ever imagined. It's a huge reality shock. You have to totally compromise yourself. I can't see anything in the future for me. My biggest fear is that five years from now I'll be bald, fat, at the same menial job, alone, and still watching life pass me by through the windows of my dad's two-bedroom. I'm hating life."

Tom Rivera grew up in an impoverished household with parents who made him feel like he had to carry the weight of the family. "They expected great and promising things from me. Pressure.

The fear built inside of me. I was terrified of the future, lost and confused," Tom says. "College was a strange time for me. I had a few friends and no relationships, and I began to have questions about myself. I thought because no girl ever showed any interest in me, I was ugly or a total geek. I wished I was someone else. After graduation, I didn't know what to do with myself. A friend suggested grad school and I agreed. Everything seemed to be getting better: I would get my master's, get a good job, and get money. Things don't always go as planned."

Partway through graduate school, Tom developed a rare disease that shook up his life. He tried working at two jobs over a six-month period, but hasn't had a "real job" since. "I just didn't care, I guess. I went to some interviews, but my meekness and weak job record didn't impress anyone. I stayed with my aging parents and just turned into a veggie. I gave up on life. Depressed, yes, but not suicidal. I had dreams—getting a job, being happy—but they never materialized. I didn't want to work in an office because I fear what others think of me (virgin, weirdo), and it was too embarrassing. I sank into a deathlike emotional state. Just blank. My fears seem to be growing daily. I'm 32, a minority male with hardly any working record or experiences and a disease," Tom says.

But Tom also has a deeper secret that he says has haunted him since childhood. He has kept this secret from all but a few anonymous Internet friends. "I've wondered if I shouldn't have been born a girl. There, I said it. I have cross-dressed since junior high. I thought of becoming a female impersonator, but I realized I didn't fit (manly face and I could never tell my family). Disappointment again. I'm not a TG (transgenderist) but a TV (transvestite). I still like women (surprise!). What a messed-up mind," he says. "I have little work experience, no sexual life, a strange hobby, a skinny, weak body. I will likely die of a painful disease. I have a high level of education but no real hopes. I have enough emotional baggage for Imelda Marcos–sized suitcases."

Currently, Tom feels paralyzed by the questions he can't stop asking himself. "I observe all that goes on around me. I just don't participate. I live sheltered for now but with huge decisions awaiting me. What do I do for an income, where will I live, should I bother trying to find a relationship with someone? Should I get professional help (please hold down the applause) for my fear, low self-esteem, gender ID problem? Heck, I never learned to drive! I am lazy and unmotivated," he says. "It is a long and difficult journey ahead of me. I must not fail this time. I can't afford to anymore. So will I ever be happy?"

Simplify Your Life

MENTOR: Kelly Johnston
AGE: 30
I WISH I'D KNOWN AT 27 THAT "things could improve so much in so little time."

In *Quarterlife Crisis,* Kelly Johnston, from Reno, Nevada, discussed the period in her life when she disliked herself, when happiness seemed like such a remote possibility that she became clinically depressed. She said back then, "I would think about my peers, all happy, carefree, and mellow, and I would just curl up and cry because I felt like I was the only person who was finding this time of life so damn hard." When a doctor diagnosed Kelly with depression, she said, "I thought, 'That couldn't be me. I was never like that.' And then I realized that that's what this transition had turned me into: this sad, antisocial person whom I myself didn't even like."

Kelly took antidepressants for a few months, in case her problem was chemical and she needed to get her wiring back on track. But she says there were other factors that helped her more than the antidepressants, which at least calmed the sense of urgent panic she felt when she thought about her future. One was learning that the frenzied way she doubted and questioned herself were normal for a twentysomething. "The other thing that helped was that I stripped my life down to the basics. I found that when I was feeling so horrible about myself, I suddenly didn't care anymore about extraneous things. The most important thing to me, my number one goal, became to find my happiness. This involved taking a long look at my life and making changes quickly."

Kelly quit her job. She cut out of her life the people, including an old friend, who made her feel worse about herself. She stopped forcing herself to socialize when she didn't want to. Instead, she only did the things that made her happy. She took long walks, worked out at the gym, spent most of her time with her boyfriend and family, and gradually got to know herself again. Now, three years later, Kelly says she wouldn't be able to recognize the person she was at 27. "I love my life now, and I'm happy. As I got in touch with the self I had lost amid the downward spiral of roaring doubts and pressures, I came to realize that I had made my life too complicated," she says. "If you don't like yourself or aren't happy, my advice is to simplify your life so that the only things that take up your time are things that can put you on a path to being happy again. Then, once you're at peace with yourself, you can build up a new life from there. My life now is a mix of old and new: same boyfriend, but new job, same close relationship with my family, but new friends, new activities, and a new attitude about myself and the adult I'll be that I never would have envisioned three years ago."

Believe in Yourself

MENTOR: Michael Coviello
AGE: 25
I WISH I'D KNOWN AT 21 THAT "true happiness and strength come from inside our hearts and not through others."

"I think the answer to that question is yes, I will be happy with my life, but for a long time, I didn't know if I ever would be," says Michael Coviello, a 2001 graduate of Marist College. "I celebrated my 25th birthday this year, the milestone twentysomethings dread—but not me. I felt I was given new freedom: for the first time in my life, I had nothing to prove to my peers, family, or friends. It was like a huge burden had been lifted from my shoulders."

When Michael was in college, he had difficulty fitting in with his classmates and couldn't understand why he didn't share their perspectives on life. "I was going through my Quarterlife Crisis during the years that should have been the best of my life. I was depressed, didn't know who I was, where I was going, or what I was good at. When I was 20, I was in a deep depression because I had lost two of my closest friends, was doing poorly in school, lost my work ethic on the job, and had no desire to keep going. Without happiness, it seemed better to go off into the permanent world of sleep. These problems almost led to the end of my life. I got professional treatment, and if hadn't been for that, I would never have gotten through my personal crisis. After about a year of that tough period, the sun came out. I changed my major in school, learned I have a remarkable ability in understanding and relating to others, and finally associated with those who believed in me. This helped me find happiness," he says. "Since I graduated, I've had ups and downs. I learned I have symptoms of Asperger's syndrome, a form of high-functioning autism, and that my depression, social problems, and interests are all connected to it. To finally learn what was wrong with me not only made me a happy person, but I also learned what I was good at, who I am, what I want to do with my life, and where it's leading me."

Michael's life now is entirely different than the one he nearly ended in college. He pursues varied interests: he works with a Web site devoted to ending school bullying, studies to prepare to pursue a master's degree in public history, and writes on the side. "The aspects of my life that make me happy now that didn't before are having effective strategies to combat loss, sadness, and frustration, having a positive attitude in times of defeat along with knowing I did my best, using my desire to keep learning and growing as a person, sticking to what I believe in, and learning it's okay to ask for help when I need it," he says. "Getting professional treatment, associating myself with the right group of people, and never giving up all helped me come to terms with myself. I also have a reason to live: the most important thing I learned was how much I loved my family and friends, and growing into the role of loving myself makes me not want to end my life now. On my 25th birthday, I made a promise that I would try to help those who feel alone and abandoned. Believe in yourself. If someone like me, who's had the odds heavily stacked against him for many years, can find true happiness and overcome a Quarterlife Crisis or any other deficit in my life, then I think anyone can."

Let People In

MENTOR: Brad Kennedy
AGE: 38
I WISH I'D KNOWN AT 24 THAT "the way you can come undone and the way you can move yourself in a more positive direction are both like powerful domino effects.

"When I was in my mid-20s, I learned that inattention to what you're not doing a good job of can unexpectedly unravel even the most basic good things that are around you, a vicious kind of downward spiral," says Brad Kennedy, a graduate of the University of California. "At 24, I was already personally at sea before a disaster struck. It was a unique kind of disaster, but that's also around the age where some kinds of disasters can strike people for the first time. You're old enough then, for example, for relatives to start dying."

For seven years, throughout college and afterward, Brad had lived with his best friend, a guy with whom he was "eerily close." When they were 24, his friend had to move to a different area to be closer to his job. At about 5:30 one morning, Brad's phone rang continuously. It was someone calling about his best friend. "He was stabbed last night," the friend told Brad. "He didn't make it." "I went and laid down for several hours, staring out the window, devoid of any reaction—just blank. When the other guys, who were all close to him, woke up, I told them and they burst out crying, saying things like 'Oh, god,' placing phone calls. I just kept lying there. I finally called his mother. She said, 'I don't know how I'll live the rest of my life,' and I told her I didn't know how I would, either."

Brad returned to work and accelerated his already breakneck workaholic pace by simultaneously accepting a book contract. He refused to talk about his friend or the murder. "I figured if I worked all the time, and never talked about it, it might kind of go away. But my imagined version of his death and the exchanges with his mother played over and over in my head. Friends I hadn't talked to since college tried to reach me, but I chose to live like a total isolate, not even taking phone calls from them. I broke up with a girlfriend and wouldn't go out at night with the other guys. I'm sure I was depressed, and slept very little. The publisher of the publication I worked at told my boss that I seemed to be 'walking around in a daze,'" Brad says. "One day, one of the guys' fathers, a psychiatrist, came for a visit from the East Coast. He came into my room and sat down. He asked me if I was talking to anyone about it and asked if I would like to talk to him. I said no, remembering that one of my favorite writers, Nabokov, called psychiatrists 'witch doctors' who try put complicated people in simple boxes. I hadn't even ever once cried over my friend. The father said, 'You're making a mistake' when he left my room."

Brad remained in this state of suspended animation for an entire year. One night he finally agreed to go out with his roommates to see the movie *Boyz N the Hood*. The movie was about two friends growing up in a city with one of the highest national rates of gang violence. "Near the end, there's a brutally violent and tragic scene which I remember precisely," Brad says. Gang members follow two close friends and shoot one of them, who is dead by the time his friend carries him home. "I walked straight out and home, shaking, basically having some kind of mini-breakdown. It was the first time I had cried since childhood. That was when I knew I wasn't all right, and that if you try to deal with a disaster by ignoring it, you're likely to see that all unravel in one ugly instant."

Brad devoted the next several months to turning his life around. When he opened up to a friend at work, the friend, a marathon runner, came in the next day with running shoes that he tossed into Brad's office. "He hauled me out into these salt flats by the San

Francisco Bay at lunch every day for a six-mile hard run. We talked while we ran, about my friend, funny things I remembered, how he died. I could feel how therapeutic it was to talk about it. I slept better at night. My friend's psychiatrist dad had been exactly right," Brad says. "I got better, plus the success of the publication I was at led me to a much better job. One domino leads to another. All of these positive things came from continuing to work hard, and the quality of the people who were around me. Other people are the key to getting many of the things that people want, and they can help solve really tough problems."

Happiness Is Just Part of the Package

MENTOR: Pam Hess
AGE: 36

I WISH I'D KNOWN AT 25 THAT "happiness is not an end state but a pleasant accident; it comes and goes, and it always comes back again. And what I experience in between is actually more critical to who I become."

"For this question I must refer you to the entire seven seasons of *Buffy the Vampire Slayer,* which addresses this issue brilliantly," says Pam Hess. "Buffy explored the fundamental, albeit somewhat depressing, truth that despite popular belief, life isn't 'supposed' to be easy or fun. It's a constant struggle to do what's right and to love despite pain and fear. The revolutionary thing about Buffy is the assertion that life often sucks beyond the telling for everyone, and happiness is what you snatch in between the sucking—the fear, the isolation, the self-doubt, the danger. The show's creator put it this way: 'Ultimately, the world is a monstrous, terrible place, and anyone that can live in it is a hero.' Contrary to what magazines, television, and movies tell you, happiness isn't something to be expected but to be savored; it's the exception rather than the rule."

Pam adapted the message of the show to reform her own attitude toward happiness. For her, she decided that happiness isn't a given—it's a privilege. "I think happiness as a goal is overrated and certainly oversold. Happiness is ephemeral and should be no more embraced than sadness, anger, or whatever. Life is just living; breathing in and out, loving people as much as you can, trying to create something, trying to achieve something. Making happiness an end in itself is self-defeating because it's so conditional. Try instead to live according to principles that mean something to you, and to understand and appreciate that life keeps throwing all manner of crap your way, in addition to the happy times. It's all valuable; it's all part of the ride. You become who you are because of the hard times, not the easy ones."

Pam is surprised that she looks back on a tough time she had a few years ago with a sense of nostalgia. "It was a trying time on a basic level: dealing with the September 11th terrorist attacks (I worked in a building that was bombed), the sudden end of a relationship I thought was leading to marriage, two family deaths, a car accident, financial and house problems. I felt like I was on my knees, just crawling to get through each day. But now I miss it. I was keenly aware of every passing moment. Life was so overwhelming that I didn't have the luxury of living in my head and asking questions like, 'Will I ever be happy?' It was moment to moment, and though excruciating, it was absorbing and total, and I knew I was alive," she says. "I haven't been happy in the carefree way I was before all that happened, but the moments of happiness I have had since then have been very sweet. Life is a process. As Spike on *Buffy* sang, 'Life's not a song; life is just this: it's living.' And to quote another song, I refer you to the Indigo Girls: 'The less I seek the answers to these questions, the closer I am to fine.' "

Face Yourself Down

MENTOR: Gail Buchwald

AGE: 37

I WISH I'D KNOWN AT 26 THAT "the easy way to be unhappy is to love something and not let yourself have it."

There were a few times in Gail Buchwald's 20s and early 30s when she wondered if she would ever be happy. The first was when she was 26. She was working as a marketer for a small company run by a "crazy male chauvinist pig," stuck in a four-year relationship with a man she didn't want to marry, and sick of moving; she'd moved seven times in four years because her group house of six friends constantly relocated. "Enter the comparing mind: I had an identical twin sister in medical school and friends in grad school. They were on a track and their track was almost over. Where was my track? It was emptiness. I was flipping out. I was reaching a dead end in my job and I had no idea what I wanted to do. I was miserable and lonely. It was like, 'Where do I go from here?' I felt I wasn't a real adult yet. Other people were like, 'Well, your twin sister is about to graduate from medical school.' "

Tired of crying every day, Gail, who had never tried therapy before, decided to see a psychiatrist. As soon as she walked into the room, a stereotypically dim, dingy room in which an older man sat with his notepad behind his desk, she had her doubts. "What seems to be the problem?" he asked her.

Through tears, she explained her issues. "I'm having a midlife crisis," she said.

He laughed at her. "Well, you don't look middle aged to me, so I don't think you're having a midlife crisis."

"I had such hope that he was going to fix me, but he really didn't," Gail says now. "A midlife crisis was the only way I could describe what I was going through. Everything had gone funky. When I left his office, I decided I needed a track. The parental voice in my head said, 'Keep up your education.' I listened to all the voices in my head that said what I should and shouldn't do. So I picked business, a degree no one could argue with."

Gail applied to one business school, Wharton, arguably the best in the country, and got in. She started her first year, "and guess what happened? I was miserable again because I had listened to the 'shoulds,' " she says. "But by the second year, I started to find my little niche. No matter where you are or how unhappy you are, there is some comfy little hole you can snuggle up in. I had to look for it. The minute I stopped taking finance classes, suddenly I was doing stuff I enjoyed, there were people I liked, there was a stray kitten in the neighborhood that I played with, and I started to feel like myself again. I decided to major in marketing and to move off campus where the other artsy types lived—little decisions, nothing radical. But those little decisions were part of what made me happy."

Confused and overwhelmed again as she neared graduation, Gail sifted through job offers from marketing and management consulting companies. Her friends encouraged her to make lists: pros and cons, point systems, scales to help her make her decision. She chose a marketing job. Finally she was on her "track." "I had all the things I thought would make me happy: a degree, a job, MBA, nice apartment, friends. I had money, I was living in the same city with my MD twin sister, and the comparing mind could sleep because I got the golden degree. But I hated the job. I was working eleven hours a day in a little cubicle. Everyone was surprised when I left, but I felt like a hamster on a wheel, going round and round. Now I know that when you have to do so many things with your head to make a decision, it's not the path to happiness," she says.

In her new marketing job, Gail was content with the job and its lifestyle for two years. "Then a door closed. (I later learned that when you think a door is closing, it's really opening.) I found out I was going to be transferred to New Jersey with a promotion, and all the shoulds came back. Suddenly I had to make a decision. For a couple years I had been content, so I didn't have to ask the hard questions. With all the little Band-Aids you can put on all the little pains, I hadn't had to ask what was important," she says. "I said no and didn't know what I was going to do. I remember my mother was upset. But it was the first time I looked a big looming should right in the face and said no. That's part of being happy, learning to not listen to the voices in your head that say, 'Should.' Of all the dark moments, that was the darkest, at age 33. The way I think of it is, depending on how you treat the wound, it'll open up again. If you just Band-Aid it, it'll open more. There was something in my life I had been suppressing through the decisions I was making. The more I tried to avoid it, the more it was building. This time I couldn't just walk into a shrink's office, hear him say no, and pick something new out to do."

In what Gail calls the "bravest time" of her life, she didn't run away from her problems. With a severance package that could sustain her for six months, she didn't rush. Instead, she let herself feel everything she had avoided thinking about: that her MBA was a waste, that she was disappointing people she loved. "I didn't seek comfort in bars, retail therapy (shopping), or say, 'Let's have a baby,' or go running. I didn't turn to all the addictions. For the first time, instead of reaching for something to make it all go away, I just kind of sat there in it, miserable. I felt the feelings coming up. I had to deal with my childhood, sadness, things I'd forgotten since my father had died. Feelings I hadn't confronted because when you go to work in the morning, you can't have certain feelings," she says. "My yoga teacher told me to think about everything I'd ever done and to come up with five to ten things that lit up my life. For me, it was taking a brisk walk in the fall, crunching leaves with a dog, playing with the kitten from downstairs, singing with my older sister. Nothing fancy. My teacher said to do at least one of those things every day. So I sang every day. I began to write because I always enjoyed it, just to express myself. I tried to make space in every day to do something that would light me up. And I repeated it."

Gail saw immediate results; she suddenly felt much better about her life. "The main thing was not running outward to find the Band-Aid at a store, gym, bar, or bakery, but about running inward, about going into the little deep spots inside me, trying to get to know myself better, and resisting the temporary fixes. Sitting longer with myself. I created a bulletin board that I called my wall of inspiration. It was made up of little things that meant something to me, whether a Ghandi quote or something my older sister said. I also started cutting cords. I let go of friendships that weren't serving me well anymore. There was a lot of pain cutting loose from parental expectations, but I decided I couldn't be close to certain people right then because sometimes the people you love aren't able to support you in the things that you need."

Gail's yoga teacher stepped in again and told her about an outlook that would change Gail's life. She said to think of a pilot navigating his course by depending on a little black box on the airplane dashboard, and the only way the pilot knows he's on course is that when he's off course, the box bleeps. "The only way I could find my course was by being off course and listening to the little black box. For most of my life, I had listened to the shoulds, voices in my head coming from parents or society. So I started to listen to the little black box, but every direction I went, it told me was wrong. I was offered marketing jobs for a lot of money, but the box was like, 'Nope. Sucks,'" Gail says.

At about that time, Gail realized that most of the activities that lit up her life had something to do with an animal. "The people I wanted to go visit, I realized, I wanted to see them to go play with their pets. Whenever things started to look up, there was a furry little creature somewhere. When I fought with my parents as a kid, I'd go cuddle with a stray cat. You put these things out of your head when you're like, 'I know what I need.' Then I came across animal welfare as a career and my little black box was screaming silent. I was an animal lover all my life, frustrated by my own inadequacy because I didn't think I was responsible enough to care for a pet. The easy way to be unhappy is to love something and not let yourself have it."

For several weeks Gail looked on the Internet and in newspapers to find an animal welfare job before she realized that she would have to create a job for herself. She decided that the difficult part of her ordeal was over, and if she was lucky enough to figure out what she wanted to do, then she owed it to herself to try to find the job that would afford her that opportunity. Her mother said she was turning down stable jobs and "talking crazy" about going to work with animals. When Gail asked a friend, "Am I crazy that this is what I want to do?" he responded, "Real people out there have those jobs." Gail decided to meet them. She visited animal organizations across the country to network. She attended lectures and seminars and afterward approached the speakers and asked them their life stories. She found there were several "switchers," people who found their course slowly and painfully, who, like Gail, gave up financial gratification for a different kind of reward. She called and e-mailed the speakers and gradually started to make friends.

Meanwhile, she stretched the six-month severance package through a year. She didn't buy clothing or go out to dinner, and worked out in the park instead of at a gym. "There were moments when I thought, 'Oh my God, this is going to be the time when I have to go to a marketing company and beg for the job offer back.' "

During the course of that year, Gail had two informational interviews with people in the ASPCA. The MBA she'd dismissed as a waste caught the eye of the ASPCA president, who called her in to meet with him. He told her he had two jobs open and asked her which one she'd prefer. Gail replied that neither one was "a perfect fit." Surprised, the president asked her what she wanted to do, and she told him: social marketing and outreach that aimed to change people's attitudes toward their pets. A few days later he created the job, and Gail was a director of a new ASPCA program. Now a vice president, Gail says she is in the most gratifying position of her life. She oversees a local service and outreach program, an animal shelter, and a fleet of mobile veterinary clinics.

"I'm very happy now. I know now that if I hadn't gotten good and miserable, I wouldn't have gotten good and happy," she says. "Did everything else in my life fall into place? No. It's always a juggling act. Where you put your focus is what grows. I focused on my lifework. It was important to focus on my values so I could wake up happy in the morning. Then I had to rebuild relationships in the spaces that grew between me and the people I loved. Happiness isn't static. You're always going to make adjustments in your course, and the little black box will tell you what you need to focus on. Part of having happiness is having that balance. I'll probably have some other darkness, but at least now I know that when it happens, it will serve as an opening to the next growth phase. The light after the darkness is so bright that it's worth hanging out in the darkness for a while."

More Ways to Conquer

I chose to end this section and this book with Gail's story because it encompasses so many of the issues addressed in previous sections. Gail went through issues including doing something she loved versus making enough money, completely changing directions, hating work, giving up on a job, considering grad school, feeling like school was a waste, settling with a romantic partner, not knowing what she wanted, finding her passion, starting over, living alone, feeling stuck, dealing with people's expectations, comparing, and feeling overwhelmed. Gail's story shows that you can work through *all* of these issues, one by one, sometimes so slowly it's painful, and still come out happier, with your life changed for the better. That you can be hit with many of these issues at once and yet learn to confront them head-on. That happiness is possible even when it seems like you have to wade through so many layers to get there.

Many of Gail's strategies can help twentysomethings who aren't happy or don't like themselves. Among other suggestions, I'd like to first reiterate one of Gail's in particular, because variations of it worked for a few of the mentors:

Make a List
Write down ten things that light up your life. Do at least one of them every day. This is how Gail was able to find the core of who she was and how she eventually was able to piece together the clues that would lead to the happy life she leads now.

Strip Down to Basics
Kelly's back-to-basics mentality might be helpful if you're experiencing the issues involved with the questions in this chapter. By

simplifying your life and stripping away unnecessary pressures, you can find the things that matter most to you and rebuild your life around those things.

Look Through Your Own Eyes

If you don't like who you are, it's also worth asking yourself, "Whose eyes am I looking through?" Are you judging yourself through the eyes of the people who ignored you in high school? The parents who expected you to be a doctor? The college class-mates who assume you'll take certain roads? To know that you love yourself unconditionally, you need to see yourself clearly through your own eyes. To do this, you may have to distance your-self from your low self-esteem. It sounds paradoxical to the idea of looking at yourself through your own eyes, but try pretending that you're a good friend of yourself, someone who loves and admires you. Then praise your life through the eyes of that imaginary friend. While the real you might be a perfectionist who sees little benefit in, say, your job unless it leads to quick promotions, the imaginary friend, whose attitude is more relaxed, might point out that you're learning excellent skills that will serve as assets in the future, and that you have great relationships with a few of your coworkers. In other words, play devil's advocate with your self-critical voice.

Consider Your Motivations

Along the same lines, you may also need to stop and think about whether you have chosen things because you want to be considered "successful" or because they make you happy. They don't always go hand in hand. Often, as twentysomethings, we are our own harshest critics. Whether we were perfectionists in school, we might try to be perfectionists in life, and then we berate ourselves if we can't live up to those unreasonable standards. One of the most important things you can do at this point in your life is to take it easy on yourself. Stop beating yourself to a mental pulp if the life you have isn't the one you want, and instead relax, listen to your little black box, and enjoy the process of finding new goals and pursuing them. The 20s, like the decades that follow, are a time to fine-tune your life in a continual process, not a time to commit yourself to settling in certain holes and staying there forever. Because your life will constantly be changing, know that happiness *will* come, as will your success in dealing with any of the Quarter-life Crisis issues in this book.

Conclusion

During the course of writing this book, I received several e-mails from people thanking me for writing it, even though all they knew about it was the list of questions to be addressed. The e-mails were along the lines of this one, from a twentysomething who wrote, "As I was reading through the questions, a huge sense of relief flooded over me. I could identify with many of the questions you presented, and it was so nice to know that I'm not the only one struggling with these issues. I always felt so alone, not comfortable sharing my feelings with family or friends, but now I realize that I'm not alone, and soon I'll have the resource I've been searching for."

I chose the questions in this book because I believe they represent a broad range of the kinds of questions we quietly bully ourselves with—the kinds of questions we're too embarrassed or shy or scared to voice to anyone else. But these are often the very questions we *have* to address if we want to move forward in our lives. I hope that one way this book has helped you has been to show you that it's not only normal, but also common, to be asking yourself these questions. Too many of us don't know this and experience a period of depression and anxiety, like Maria, a twentysomething

I interviewed for an article on the Quarterlife Crisis a few years ago. She said back then, "Everybody else I knew seemed to be getting the kinds of jobs and lives they wanted, and I wasn't. I was afraid they would find out how clueless and apprehensive I was about my future. If I ran into someone I knew while grocery shopping, I would actually hide; I didn't want to have that 'So, what are *you* doing' conversation and let anybody know that I wasn't making it. I didn't want them to think I was a loser." That right there is why I decided to write books on the Quarterlife Crisis, why it was so important to name the Quarterlife Crisis in the first place. I write about the Quarterlife Crisis because I want people to know that if you feel that way, if your 20s aren't the party you expected them to be, you are *not* a loser and you are not alone.

I hope the mentors in this book have helped you to go at least one step further by giving you the tools and/or the motivation to enhance, improve, or change your life. I hope that, among the diverse group, there was at least one mentor you could relate to or whose suggestions seemed personally tailored to your issues. I hope you're now ready to take the next steps—the ones that will finally allow you to conquer your Quarterlife Crisis.

But if not, here are a few more ideas. First, in the past few years, a number of Quarterlife Crisis support groups have sprouted in various corners of the world. After sitting in on a few of these meetings, I've come to the conclusion that while it's nice to have these groups' compassionate companionship, they could be doing more. Whether you have a support group or simply a group of friends who want help working through their issues, here's an idea for how to make these kinds of get-togethers truly impact your life. Instead of meeting simply to chat over a meal, use the gathered multiple brainpower to your advantage.

Approach these get-togethers not just to talk about each other's problems but, more important, specifically to *solve* them. Devote each meeting, or each half hour of a meeting, to coming up with strategies to solve a member's specific problem. Pool networks. Introduce singles. Trade skills. Develop your own mentors from within the group. Air your problem, and have the others come up with a variety of ways to go about solving it. The group will come up with something—a strategy, a connection—that you hadn't thought of before. Even better, the group will give you the benefit of perspective.

Speaking of which, at the end of the first *Quarterlife Crisis,* readers heard from Irving, a then 90-year-old who put our feelings of inadequacy in perspective. As a teacher and principal, Irving spent a lifetime with students; and as a now 94-year-old, he has a lifetime's worth of advice, not to mention the reassurance that our twentysomething issues look different from a wider angle. For this book, I again turned to Irving to ask him how the worries and stresses of the 20s look from the perspective of age 94.

"People in their 20s, just as people in their teens and their 30s, will make mistakes, but they should know it's not the end of the world because of the long life ahead of them. They will learn, and they won't make the same mistake twice. Just use the twenties as a learning experience. Their lives are going to be much richer for the insight into other people and their own capabilities and potentials. People in the Quarterlife Crisis have a long life ahead of them. I'd tell them not to be concerned about mistakes. There will be other ways of solving problems. That's why I say mistakes made at that age are not serious and could be corrected. For example, if you choose the wrong course in education, it could be corrected even the next year. There isn't only one way, and if you lose that way, it's not the end of the world. There are always other ways of meeting your challenges. There are different challenges when you reach each decade. A failure to meet a challenge at one of those times isn't life-threatening," Irving says. "There are always questions, but the questions at 25 become insignificant when you reach 35. Eventually you'll consider the questions trivial, not life-changing."

Perhaps most important, Irving tells us that while so many things in our lives seem so dire, urgent, and monumental now, the choices we make won't seem so crucial when we have decades of distance behind us. "When you're 94," Irving says, "the 20s look very far back; they would almost fit into a history book. The period of the 20s is a small blip on the chart of life. It's such a distant memory. You remember the times, whether difficult or easy, and you wonder how you survived the anxieties and the worries that you may have had in reaching your goals. But if you persist in your endeavors, you're bound to realize your goals."

I hope this book has at least taught you that, as Irving says, there are myriad ways to reach your goals, and I hope it has inspired you to strive for them. Just as important, I hope the stories you've just read have proven to you that having Quarterlife Crisis issues doesn't mean you're weird, flawed, or spoiled. What these doubts and questions mean is that your self is giving you signs that you need to make a change, whether in action or attitude. The point of this book was to give you the motivation, inspiration, advice, and, in many cases, specific steps to help you accept this need to change and to then make the necessary adjustments. A Quarterlife Crisis isn't something through which you have to suffer stoically, waiting passively for it to end. You can break down these complex questions into simple steps to follow, bit by bit, until you triumph over your fears. And then not only will you be able to work through your own Quarterlife Crisis, but also, just as important, you'll be able to mentor other twentysomethings to conquer their Quarterlife Crises as well.

Acknowledgments

I am so fortunate to have the parents I do. Their love, wisdom, support, guidance, insights, kindness, and encouragement continue to be invaluable to me at every stage of my life, both professionally and personally. It is impossible to adequately convey in these pages how much I appreciate them and everything they have done for me.

I am similarly grateful to the rest of my family. Missy, Andrew, and Dave make sure I'm laughing, even when I'm working too hard for my own good. Their humor, ideas, and blunt candor keep me going on a daily basis. Thank you to Irving, whose shrewd counsel and priceless perspective have helped countless twentysomethings through trying times. He is the only 94-year-old I know of whom I can truly say is wise beyond his years.

My agent Paula Balzer has been a great friend and fantastic resource since she took on my first book five years ago. I'm thankful for the contributions she makes to every book I write, many of which go much beyond the call of duty. I am thoroughly indebted to Susan Petersen Kennedy, who placed this book with Michelle Howry. A joy to work with, Michelle has been the ideal editor for *Conquering Your Quarterlife Crisis*; the obvious energy and

226 Acknowledgments

incredible care she took truly made this book the best a reader could want.

I also thank the hundreds of twenty- and thirtysomethings who contributed to this book, whether or not their stories made the last cut (many stories that didn't can be found on the Web site below). Their honesty and terrific, hard-earned advice will undoubtedly make many of their peers' lives better.

Finally, I am always grateful to the readers, who continue to e-mail me with comments and suggestions at *www.alexandrarobbins.com.*

Index

About the Author

New York Times bestselling author Alexandra Robbins regularly speaks to groups about twenty- and thirtysomething issues. To contact her about scheduling a lecture, please visit *www.alexandrarobbins.com*.

Robbins's books include *Pledged: The Secret Life of Sororities* (April 2004), *Secrets of the Tomb: Skull and Bones, the Ivy League, and the Hidden Paths of Power* (September 2002), and *Quarterlife Crisis: The Unique Challenges of Life in Your Twenties* (May 2001). Formerly on the staff of *The New Yorker*, Robbins's work has appeared in several publications, including *Vanity Fair, The New Yorker, The Atlantic Monthly, The Washington Post, Teen Vogue, Chicago Tribune, Cosmopolitan, PC,* and *USA Today*.

Robbins frequently appears in the national media on shows such as "60 Minutes," "The Today Show," "The Oprah Winfrey Show," CBS's "The Early Show," "Paula Zahn Now," "The Diane Rehm Show," and networks including CNN, NPR, the BBC, VH1, MSNBC, CNBC, C-SPAN, and the History Channel.